# Practice for the New York State Mathematics Test

## Grade 4

**Harcourt Brace & Company**

Orlando • Atlanta • Austin • Boston • San Francisco • Chicago • Dallas • New York • Toronto • London

*www.hbschool.com*

# CONTENTS

Harcourt Brace School Publishers

Name _____

**1** Angela and Tom set up a race course for their bicycles. The course goes around their neighborhood. It begins and ends at Angela's house.

Which is a reasonable distance for a bicycle race?

Ⓐ 2 inches

Ⓑ 2 feet

Ⓒ 2 yards

Ⓓ 2 miles

**Test Taking Tips**

Which unit is commonly used to measure distances on streets?

---

**2** Terri built a pattern with groups of counters. It looked like this.

If this pattern continues, how many coins will be in her next group?

Ⓕ 12 coins

Ⓖ 13 coins

Ⓗ 14 coins

Ⓘ 15 coins

**Test Taking Tips**

What pattern do you see?

Grade 4 • Harcourt Brace School Publishers

New York Test Prep

Name _____

**3** Cassie saw that her score on a video game was 4053. When she looked again, the 5 had changed to an 8. By how much had her score changed?

**4053**

Explain your reasoning.

_____

_____

_____

_____

Test Taking Tips

What do you know about place value that will help you solve this problem and explain your reasoning?

---

**4** Sort these shapes into two groups.

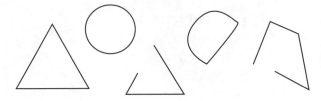

On the lines below, draw the groups. Explain your sorting rules.

_____

_____

_____

Test Taking Tips

Do all the shapes have straight lines? Are they all closed?

Grade 4 • Harcourt Brace School Publishers

**5** Mario is taking the bus to his aunt's house. The bus only takes exact change. The fare is 75¢. Mario has these coins.

Think • Solve • Explain
Long Answer

**Test Taking Tips**

What coins does Mario have?

What does "exact change" mean?

Grade 4 • Harcourt Brace School Publishers

**5** Use Mario's coins.

Show two ways to make exact change for 75¢.

**Test Taking Tips**

How can you check to see if your answers are right?

What are the fewest coins that Mario can use for bus fare? Explain how you decided.

_____

_____

_____

_____

_____

_____

_____

_____

_____

**1** When Simon finished cleaning his room, his building blocks were piled neatly in the corner as shown below.

How many blocks are in his pile?

Ⓐ 10 blocks

Ⓑ 16 blocks

Ⓒ 17 blocks

Ⓓ 24 blocks

Test Taking Tips

Are there parts of the picture that you cannot see?

How can making a model help solve the problem?

**2** Li-Ping and her brother Sam were playing video games. Li-Ping scored 2,398 points. Sam said, "Guess what my score is. It is 1,000 points more than yours."

How many points did Sam have?

Ⓕ 1,398

Ⓖ 2,298

Ⓗ 3,398

Ⓘ 4,398

Test Taking Tips

How can you use place value to help solve the problem?

**3** Philip and Carlota drew these shapes for a geometry art project.

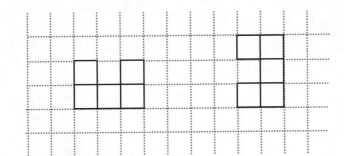

Are their shapes congruent? How do you know? Explain your reasoning.

_____

_____

_____

_____

Test Taking Tips

What does congruent mean?
What is always true about congruent figures?

**4** On Monday, March 1, three students came to Karate class. On Tuesday, March 2, six students came. On Wednesday, March 3, nine students came. This pattern continued all week. How many students came on Saturday, March 6?

| Mon.<br>Mar. 1 | Tues.<br>Mar. 2 | Wed.<br>Mar. 3 | Thurs.<br>Mar. 4 | Fri.<br>Mar. 5 | Sat.<br>Mar. 6 |
|---|---|---|---|---|---|
|  |  |  |  |  |  |

Describe a pattern in your chart.

_____

_____

Test Taking Tips

How can you complete the chart to find the pattern?

Grade 4 • Harcourt Brace School Publishers

**5** Look at the shape of Wendy's gingerbread cookie house. The roof is a triangle. The sides of the triangle have the same measure. The triangle has a perimeter of 18 inches. Wendy is going to outline her house with ribbon. How much ribbon will she need to go all the way around?

How long is one side of the triangle? How do you know?

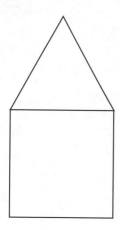

Remember that perimeter is the distance around an object.

Grade 4 • Harcourt Brace School Publishers

**5** Explain how you solved the problem. Use words and pictures.

Test
Taking
Tips

How can you check to see if your answer is right?

_____

_____

_____

_____

_____

_____

Name _____

**1** Mrs. Castillo has four daughters.

Our Birthdays

| Andrea | June 8, 1994 |
| Josefina | May 23, 1992 |
| Martina | July 27, 1990 |
| Teresa | March 13, 1996 |

Who is the oldest child?

Ⓐ  Andrea

Ⓑ  Josefina

Ⓒ  Martina

Ⓓ  Teresa

Test Taking Tips

Which of these years came before all the other years?

**2** What number is missing in the following number sentence?

$$3 + (4 + 7) = (3 + 4) + \underline{\hspace{1cm}}$$

Ⓕ  3

Ⓖ  4

Ⓗ  7

Ⓘ  11

Test Taking Tips

What property of addition does the number sentence show?

Name _____

**3** Judy drew some stairs on dot paper. She decided to make more stairs going the other way. She will flip her design. Draw the flip of Judy's design.

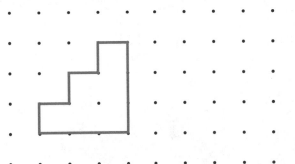

On the lines below explain why the two designs are symmetrical.

_____

_____

**Test Taking Tips**

What does symmetrical mean?

What is true of all symmetrical figures?

---

**4** Jonathan went into the store to get a gallon of milk for his mother.

He gave the cashier $5 to pay for the milk. He received $0.57 in change. Use ESTIMATION to help Jonathan explain to the cashier how much change he should have received.

_____

_____

**Test Taking Tips**

What is the price for one gallon of milk?

How can you use rounding to estimate the correct change?

Name _____

**5** William, Thomas, and Beth were doing a set of 12 homework problems. At the end of 30 minutes, William had three-fourths finished, Thomas had 6 problems done, and Beth had two-thirds finished.

Draw pictures to show the number of problems each student had finished.

**Test Taking Tips**

How can you use the picture to show how many problems William had completed?

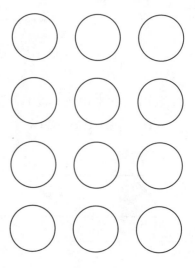

Name _____

**5** Who had the most problems finished?

_____

Explain how you solved the problem.
Use pictures, words, and numbers.

**Test Taking Tips**

How can you check that your answers are correct?

William's work:

Thomas's work:

Beth's work:

Name _____

**1** Enrico's favorite T.V. program comes on at 5:00 P.M. His sister's favorite program is on $2\frac{1}{2}$ hours later and lasts 30 minutes. At what time does his sister's favorite program end?

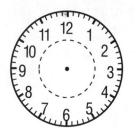  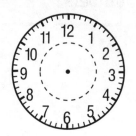

Ⓐ 5:30 P.M.

Ⓑ 7:30 P.M.

Ⓒ 8:00 P.M.

Ⓓ 8:30 P.M.

Test Taking Tips

How does showing each time help solve the problem?

---

**2** How many lines of symmetry are in this hexagon?

Ⓕ 2

Ⓖ 3

Ⓗ 4

Ⓘ 6

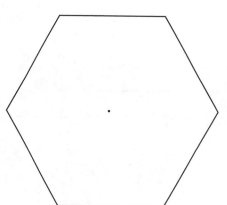

Test Taking Tips

What math words do you need to know?

Name _____

**3** Eric is the manager of the Must See Video Store. He wants to buy 30 new videos for the store. He surveyed his customers to learn their favorite type of movie.

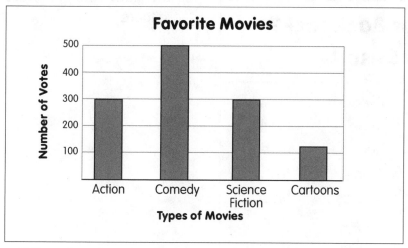

What kinds of movies should he buy?

_____

Explain how you used the data from the survey to make your decision.

_____

_____

Test Taking Tips

What does each bar of the graph show?

---

**4** Sabrina says that there are exactly three ways to make 45 cents without using any pennies. Is she correct?

_____

Explain your reasoning. List all the ways you can find.

_____

_____

Test Taking Tips

How will making a chart help you know if you have found all the ways?

Grade 4 • Harcourt Brace School Publishers

Name _____

**5** Mr. Toma's class took a survey to find out the most common color of the backpacks students carry. Here are the results.

How many different colors are there?

## What Color Is Your Backpack?
## Class Survey Results

| | | | |
|---|---|---|---|
| Stephanie | black | Alyssa | brown |
| Taoran | green | Angelo | black |
| Matei | black | Kamran | green |
| Rachel | blue | Alanna | red |
| Rebecca | blue | Nikolas | black |
| Monika | blue | Linnea | blue |
| Corey | black | Sophie | blue |
| Justin | brown | Jeremiah | black |
| Kurtis | green | William | green |
| Adelina | blue | Patricia | red |
| Lana | red | Tanisha | red |

Organize the results in a table.

## Class Survey Results

| Color of Backpack | Number of Students |
|---|---|
| | |
| | |
| | |
| | |
| | |

**18**

Grade 4 • Harcourt Brace School Publishers

Name _____

**5** Make a bar graph that shows the results of the survey. Be sure to

- give your graph a title
- use a scale
- tell what each bar shows
- correctly show the data

Write two statements that compare the data on backpack colors.

**Test Taking Tips**

How many different colors do the data show?

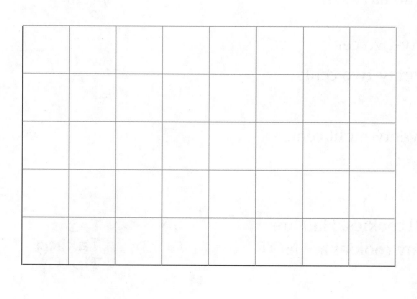

_____

_____

_____

_____

Name _____

**1** Bob made $28 mowing grass over the weekend. He gave half to his mother. He spent $4.78 for lunch.

How much money did Bob have left?

Ⓐ Ten dollars and thirty-two cents

Ⓑ Nine dollars and twenty-two cents

Ⓒ Sixteen dollars

Ⓓ Four dollars and seventy-eight cents

Test Taking Tips

How much money did Bob have when he went to lunch?

**2** Samantha has laid out 30 cookies. Half are chocolate chip. How many cookies are NOT chocolate chip?

Ⓕ 10 cookies

Ⓖ 15 cookies

Ⓗ 20 cookies

Ⓘ 25 cookies

Test Taking Tips

How can drawing a picture help you solve the problem?

Grade 4 • Harcourt Brace School Publishers

Name _____

**3** Alonzo and Janet are playing a game. If the spinner lands on a 2-digit number, Alonzo gets five points. If the spinner lands on a 1-digit number, Janet gets five points. The purpose of the game is to win 50 points.

Who is more likely to win the game?

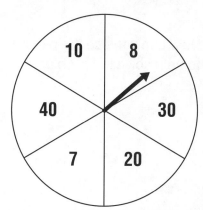

_____

On the lines below, explain how you decided.

_____

_____

_____

Test Taking Tips

How many spaces on the spinner have a 2-digit number?

How many spaces on the spinner have a 1-digit number?

**4** Which measure is the best ESTIMATE to describe the length of the salamander?

Circle the best estimate.

    3 inches    3 miles    3 pounds

On the lines below, explain how you decided.

_____

_____

Test Taking Tips

How do you use each unit of measure?

Grade 4 • Harcourt Brace School Publishers

Name _____

**5** Jolene is setting up a store. She has 36 erasers. She wants to charge 10¢ for each eraser. She is trying to decide how many erasers to put into each package.

Test Taking Tips

Think • Solve • Explain
Long Answer

How can you use the picture to help solve the problem?

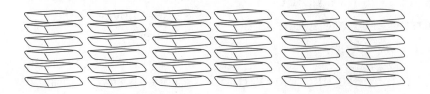

Help Jolene find three different ways to package 36 erasers with no leftovers. Record your ideas on the chart.

| Idea | Number of Erasers in 1 Package | Number of Packages | Price per Package |
|---|---|---|---|
|  |  |  |  |
|  |  |  |  |
|  |  |  |  |
|  |  |  |  |
|  |  |  |  |
|  |  |  |  |
|  |  |  |  |

New York Test Prep

Grade 4 • Harcourt Brace School Publishers

Name _____

**5** Explain how you decided how to make packages with no leftovers. Use pictures, words and numbers.

Solve • Explain • Think
Long Answer

**Test Taking Tips**

How can you make a list to solve the problem?

**1** Tonya and Brittany were setting up a race course for their pet hamsters. They want to see how far the hamsters can run in 10 seconds.

Which is the most reasonable unit to measure the distance the hamsters run in 10 seconds?

Ⓐ miles

Ⓑ square feet

Ⓒ tons

Ⓓ feet

**Test Taking Tips**

Which choices do NOT seem reasonable?

**2** Kendra and Marco drew a map of their neighborhood. How many blocks long is the perimeter of the park?

Remember: Perimeter is the distance around a shape.

Ⓕ 4

Ⓖ 6

Ⓗ 10

Ⓘ 20

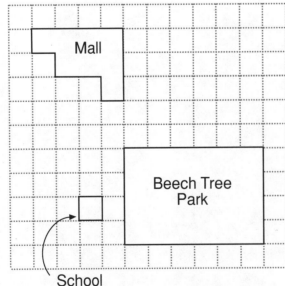

**Test Taking Tips**

How can you use the map to find the length and width of the park?

Grade 4 • Harcourt Brace School Publishers

New York Test Prep

Name _____

**Daily Practice**
**Week**
**6**

**3** Fran is buying treats for a party. There will be four people to share the treats. She wants everyone to have the same number of treats. She can buy a package of 16, 26, or 30.

30 whistles

16 balloons

26 poppers

Which package should she buy?

_____

Explain how you decided.

_____

_____

What operation will you use to solve the problem?

---

**4** Tanisha and Joel collect baseball cards. Tanisha has 569 cards. Joel has 596 cards. Who has more cards?

Show each number on the number line.

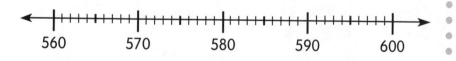

560      570      580      590      600

Write a number sentence that compares their card collections.

_____

How can a number line help you decide who has more cards?

Name _____

Daily Practice
Week
6

Think • Solve • Explain
Long Answer

Test
Taking
Tips

**5** Adam bought two snacks at the school carnival. He paid $0.06 in sales tax. When Adam gave the cashier $1.00, he received $0.20 in change.

What did Adam buy?

How can working backward help you solve the problem?

## Snacks at the Carnival

$0.29

$0.49

$0.25

$0.80

$0.45

$0.65

Name _____

**5** What did Adam buy?

_____

_____

On the lines below, explain your thinking. Use numbers and words.

_____

_____

_____

_____

**Test Taking Tips**

Think • Solve • Explain
Long Answer

How can estimation help you check that your answers are reasonable?

Grade 4 • Harcourt Brace School Publishers

**1** There is a new student in Victor's class. What are the chances that this student's birthday is in a month that starts with the letter J?

January  April  July  October
February  May  August  November
March  June  September  December

Ⓐ   1 out of 3

Ⓑ   3 out of 1

Ⓒ   3 out of 3

Ⓓ   3 out of 12

**Test Taking Tips**

What information do you need in order to solve the problem?

---

**2** Tomiwa and his team are writing a report about recycling. They found out that their city recycled one thousand two hundred three pounds of newspaper in September and nine hundred fifty-nine pounds in October.

How many pounds of newspaper were recycled in those two months?

Ⓕ   1,918 pounds

Ⓖ   1,982 pounds

Ⓗ   2,162 pounds

Ⓘ   2,406 pounds

**Test Taking Tips**

How can writing the data in standard form help solve the problem?

Name _____

**3** Louis wants to measure the amount of water in his swimming pool.

Which unit of measurement should he use, cups, pints, quarts, or gallons?

_____

Explain how you decided.

_____

_____

_____

Solve
Think
Short Answer
Explain

Test
Taking
Tips

Which measure holds more, a cup, a pint, a quart, or a gallon?

---

**4** Ricky has a riddle for his friend Marcello. There are two numbers. Their difference is 24. Their sum is 60. What are the two numbers?

_____

On the lines below, explain how you decided.

_____

_____

_____

_____

How can you use a table to organize your guess and checks for the two numbers?

Name _____

**5** Look at the quilt square Miranda designed. How many different congruent patch pieces make up the design?

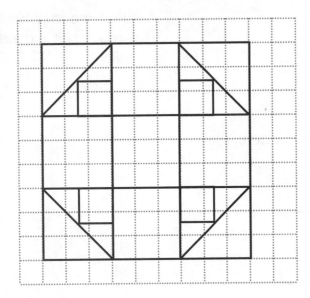

Draw each one.

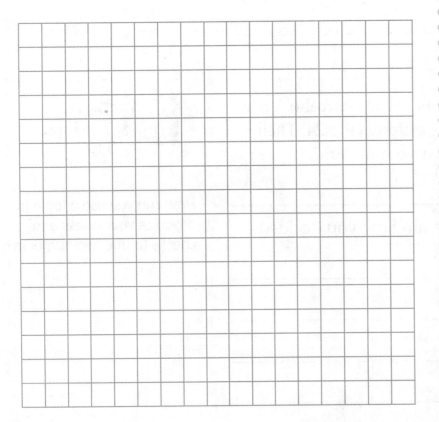

What math word do you need to know to solve the problem?

What is always true about congruent figures?

Name _____

**5** Name each figure that you found.

_____

_____

_____

_____

How can making a list of the shapes and sizes help you solve the problem?

How do you know which figures are congruent? Use pictures and words to explain your reasoning.

_____

_____

_____

_____

_____

_____

_____

Grade 4 • Harcourt Brace School Publishers

Name _____

**1** Last month a music concert was held at an auditorium with 4,000 seats. Half the auditorium was closed for repairs. The rest of the auditorium was full. The seating area is divided into sections. Each section seats 500 people.

How many SECTIONS were used?

Ⓐ 4

Ⓑ 80

Ⓒ 250

Ⓓ 2,000

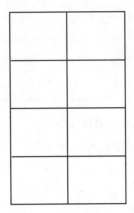

Multiple Choice
**Test Taking Tips**

How can you use the picture to solve the problem?

---

**2** Meg and Ramirez made a value chart for the letters of the alphabet.

The word HAT is worth $0.29. How much is the word WHALE worth?

Ⓕ $0.21

Ⓖ $0.23

Ⓗ $0.39

Ⓘ $0.49

**Test Taking Tips**

What information in the chart do you need to solve the problem?

| Letter | Value |
|--------|-------|
| A | 1¢ |
| B | 2¢ |
| C | 3¢ |
| D | 4¢ |
| E | 5¢ |
| F | 6¢ |
| G | 7¢ |
| H | 8¢ |
| I | 9¢ |
| J | 10¢ |
| K | 11¢ |
| L | 12¢ |
| M | 13¢ |

| Letter | Value |
|--------|-------|
| N | 14¢ |
| O | 15¢ |
| P | 16¢ |
| Q | 17¢ |
| R | 18¢ |
| S | 19¢ |
| T | 20¢ |
| U | 21¢ |
| V | 22¢ |
| W | 23¢ |
| X | 24¢ |
| Y | 25¢ |
| Z | 26¢ |

Grade 4 • Harcourt Brace School Publishers

Name _____

**3** Sam is going to visit his grandmother. He arrives at the airport at 2:00 P.M. His flight is supposed to leave at 3:10 P.M. The flight attendant announces that the departure will be delayed by 30 minutes.

How long will Sam have to wait at the airport?

_____

On the lines below, explain your reasoning.

_____

_____

**Test Taking Tips**

At what time should Sam's flight leave now?

---

**4** Which of these pictures show a slide ONLY? Circle your answer.

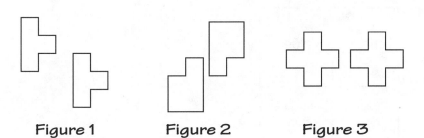

Figure 1          Figure 2          Figure 3

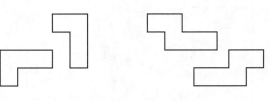

Figure 4          Figure 5

On the lines below, explain your reasoning.

_____

_____

**Test Taking Tips**

What is the difference between a slide and a turn?

Grade 4 • Harcourt Brace School Publishers

New York Test Prep

Name _____

Test
Taking
Tips

**5** Adelina and Amad are working as a team to find the word with the most points. They are using this chart.

Which letters have the most points?

### Points per Letter

| A | B | C | D | E | F | G | H | I | J | K | L | M |
|---|---|---|---|---|---|---|---|---|---|---|---|---|
| 1 | 2 | 3 | 4 | 5 | 6 | 7 | 8 | 9 | 10 | 11 | 12 | 13 |

| N | O | P | Q | R | S | T | U | V | W | X | Y | Z |
|---|---|---|---|---|---|---|---|---|---|---|---|---|
| 14 | 15 | 16 | 17 | 18 | 19 | 20 | 21 | 22 | 23 | 24 | 25 | 26 |

Find a word that is worth more points than "roadrunner."

| Letter | Value |
|--------|-------|
| R | 18 |
| O | 15 |
| A | 1 |
| D | 4 |
| R | 18 |
| U | 21 |
| N | 14 |
| N | 14 |
| E | 5 |
| R | +18 |
| Total | 128 |

| Letter | Value |
|--------|-------|
|  |  |
|  |  |
|  |  |
|  |  |
|  |  |
|  |  |
|  |  |
|  |  |
|  |  |
|  |  |
| Total |  |

**34**

Grade 4 • Harcourt Brace School Publishers

Name _____

**5** One team said, "A longer word is always worth more than a shorter word." Do you agree?

_____

Explain your thinking. Give examples of words to prove your opinion.

Test Taking Tips

How can you check that your explanation is clear and correct?

_____

_____

_____

_____

_____

_____

Name _____

**1** Which of the following shapes DOES NOT have a line of symmetry?

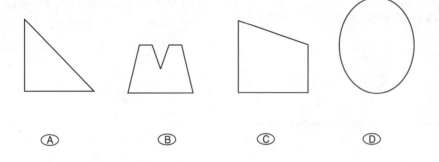

Ⓐ          Ⓑ          Ⓒ          Ⓓ

**2** Maria made a weekly calendar of her activities.

| Maria's Weekly Schedule | | |
| --- | --- | --- |
| Mon. | dance class | 4:00 – 5:15 |
| Tues. | soccer | 5:00 – 6:30 |
| Wed. | dance class | 4:00 – 5:15 |
| Thurs. | | |
| Fri. | babysit | 6:00 – 8:15 |
| Sat. | dance class | 12:15 – 1:30 |

How many minutes does she spend at dance class each week?

Reminder: 1 hour = 60 minutes

Ⓕ  75 minutes

Ⓖ  150 minutes

Ⓗ  195 minutes

Ⓘ  225 minutes

Grade 4 • Harcourt Brace School Publishers

Name _____

**3** Carlos is balancing wooden blocks. He notices that two square blocks will balance one triangle. He also notices that one triangle and one circle will balance five square blocks.

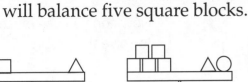

How many square blocks must Carlos use to balance one circle? Explain your thinking.

_____

_____

_____

What information does the first scale give you that can help solve the problem?

How can Carlos balance a circle WITHOUT the triangle?

**4** Joanie and Phil are playing a game like Tic Tac Toe. Three markers in a row win. Phil is using X's. It's Phil's turn. Where must he put his marker to keep from losing the game?

( __ , __ )

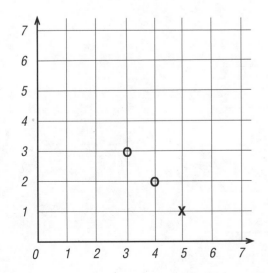

How do you name a point on a grid?

Which number do you name first, the number across or the number up?

Grade 4 • Harcourt Brace School Publishers

Name _____

**5** Mrs. Munoz's class is playing The Smallest Number Game. Arlette's team drew these number cards.

Rafael's team drew these cards.

What is the smallest number that each team can make?

Arlette _____

Rafael _____

Explain how you decided.

_____

_____

_____

_____

_____

**Test Taking Tips**

Think • Solve • Explain

Long Answer

How can you use place value to solve the problem?

Grade 4 • Harcourt Brace School Publishers

**5** In the Greatest Sum Game, can the two teams together make a SUM that is greater than 100,000?

_____

Explain how you decided.

_____

_____

_____

_____

_____

_____

_____

_____

How can you use ESTIMATION to solve the problem?

Name _____

**1** Look at Figure 1.

Which of the figures below show Figure 1 flipped to the right?

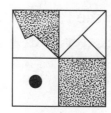

Figure 1

Test Taking Tips

How do you move a shape when you flip it?

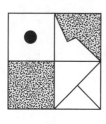

Ⓐ

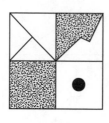

Ⓑ

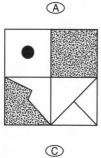

Ⓒ

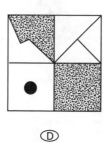

Ⓓ

---

**2** There are 40 ounces of juice in Jar A. ESTIMATE about how many ounces of juice are likely to be in Jar B.

Jar A

Jar B

Ⓕ between 40 and 60 ounces

Ⓖ between 80 and 100 ounces

Ⓗ between 100 and 120 ounces

Ⓘ between 120 and 160 ounces

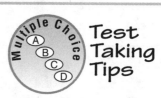

Test Taking Tips

How much fuller is Jar B than Jar A?

**40**

New York Test Prep

Name _____

**3** Jamie has started a pattern using tiles.

Square
1    Square
2    Square
3    Square
4    Square
5

How many tiles will Jamie need to make the fifth square in his pattern?

_____

Explain how you decided.

_____

_____

**4** Allen took $100.00 on his shopping trip. He bought his mom a new dress for $59.57. He bought his sister a new baseball cap for $16.19. He bought his brother a toy truck for $18.92. These prices INCLUDE sales tax.

How much change did Allen receive?

_____

Show your work below.

**Test Taking Tips**

What two steps could be used to solve this problem?

Grade 4 • Harcourt Brace School Publishers

Name _____

**5** Jacob is deciding what to wear for picture day at school. Here are his choices.

How can making an organized list help you solve the problem?

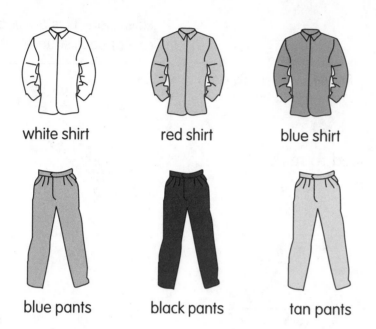

white shirt     red shirt     blue shirt

blue pants     black pants     tan pants

He is going to try them in different ways.

Name _____

**5** How many choices does Jacob have?

_____

What are they?

_____

_____

_____

_____

_____

_____

_____

How can you check that your answer is clear and complete?

Explain how you know that you have found all the possible outfits he can make.

_____

_____

_____

_____

_____

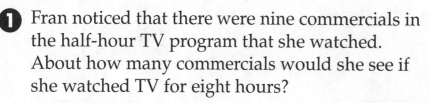

**1** Fran noticed that there were nine commercials in the half-hour TV program that she watched. About how many commercials would she see if she watched TV for eight hours?

Ⓐ Fewer than 50

Ⓑ Between 50 and 90

Ⓒ Between 90 and 125

Ⓓ More than 125

About how many commercials will there be in each full hour of programming?

**2** On July 14, the hot dog vendor expects to sell twice as many hot dogs as she sold on June 9. How many hot dogs does she expect to sell on July 14?

**Hot Dog Sales**

June 9

June 16

June 23

June 30

July 7

= 10 hot dogs

Ⓕ 11 hotdogs

Ⓖ 45 hotdogs

Ⓗ 90 hotdogs

Ⓘ 120 hotdogs

What information in the pictograph will help you solve the problem?

Grade 4 • Harcourt Brace School Publishers

Name _____

**3** Angelo was waiting to order his pizza. He noticed a pattern on the ordering chart on the wall.

   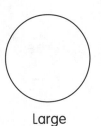

Mini      Small      Medium      Large

If the pattern continues, how many slices will there be in the Large Size Pizza?

_____

On the lines below, explain how you decided.

_____

_____

Test Taking Tips

How does the number of slices in each pizza compare to the number of slices in the next size?

---

**4** Sarah's class is selling pencils for a fund raising project. They sold 142 pencils for 20¢ each.

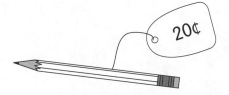

Are their total sales closer to $10, $20, $30, or $40?

_____

Explain how you decided.

_____

_____

Test Taking Tips

How can ESTIMATING help you solve the problem?

Grade 4 • Harcourt Brace School Publishers

Daily Practice
Week
11

Think • Solve • Explain
Long Answer

Test
Taking
Tips

**5** Mariel and John are making up a geometry game. They are using these shapes in their game. The object of the game is to guess the sorting rule.

Here is how they sorted the shapes.

What geometry words will help you describe the shapes in each group?

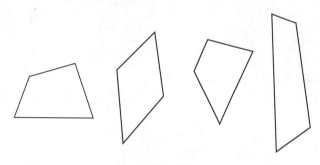

Group I

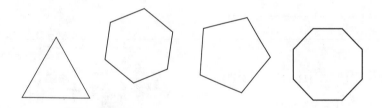

Group II

46

Grade 4 • Harcourt Brace School Publishers

Name _____

**5** Write three statements that describe the shapes in each group.

Group I

_____

_____

_____

_____

_____

How can you check that your answer is clear and complete?

Group II

_____

_____

_____

_____

_____

Name _____

**1**

William is drawing a W on grid paper. He has used ordered pairs to show these points.

(1, 6), (2, 1), (3, 4 ), (4, 1)

**Test Taking Tips**

Which number shows the position horizontally or straight across?

Which number shows the position vertically or straight up?

Where should his last point be?

- Ⓐ (4, 6)
- Ⓑ (5, 6)
- Ⓒ (6, 5)
- Ⓓ (6, 6)

**2** Kristina's mother is making a birthday cake in the shape of an octagon. She will put three small candles on each corner of the cake.

How many candles will she put on the cake?

- Ⓕ 24 candles
- Ⓖ 21 candles
- Ⓗ 16 candles
- Ⓘ 8 candles

**Test Taking Tips**

What math words do you need to know to solve the problem?

New York Test Prep

Grade 4 • Harcourt Brace School Publishers

Name _____

**3** Julian's class took a survey of peanuts in a snack pack. They made a graph of their findings.

About how many peanuts would you expect to find in a similar snack pack of peanuts?

**Number of Peanuts in a Pack**

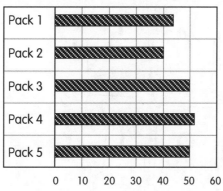

_____

On the lines below, explain how you decided.

_____

_____

What is the least number of peanuts counted in a snack pack?

What is the greatest number of peanuts found in a snack pack?

---

**4** Your team wins a point when the pointer lands on red.

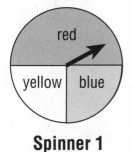

**Spinner 1**

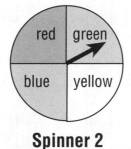

**Spinner 2**

Which spinner would give your team a better chance of winning?

_____

On the lines below, explain how you decided.

_____

_____

What fraction of each spinner is red?

Grade 4 • Harcourt Brace School Publishers

Daily Practice
Week
12

Think • Solve • Explain
Long
Answer

**Test
Taking
Tips**

**5** Shayla and Brian are playing a math game. They are using these cards.

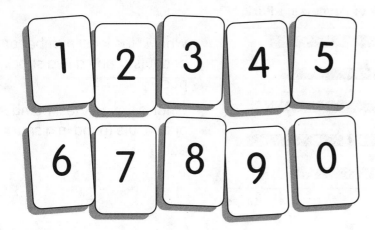

How can you arrange 6 of these cards in the addends to find the largest possible sum?

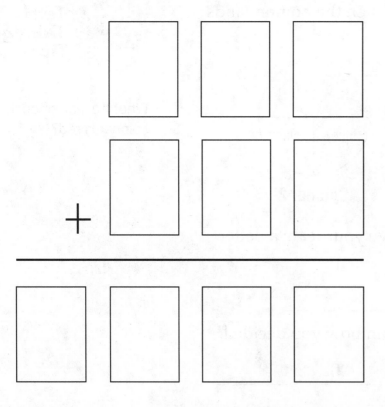

**5** What strategy did you use to make the largest sum?

On the lines below, explain how you decided.

_____

_____

_____

_____

_____

_____

_____

_____

_____

**Test Taking Tips**

How can you use place value to explain how to make the greatest sum?

Name _____

**1** In LaKeisha's city there are four tall buildings. The height of each building is shown below.

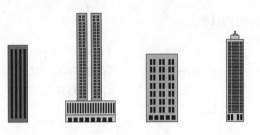

| Bank | Hotel | Offices | Apartments |
| 327 ft | 452 ft | 280 ft | 371 ft |

What is the difference in feet between the tallest building and the shortest building?

Ⓐ   91 feet

Ⓑ   125 feet

Ⓒ   172 feet

Ⓓ   732 feet

**2** How many sides are on seven hexagons?

Ⓕ   6 sides

Ⓖ   35 sides

Ⓗ   42 sides

Ⓘ   49 sides

**3** At the championship basketball game, Terry's team scored 77 points. All 11 players got a chance to play and score some points.

| Points Scored | |
| --- | --- |
| Mark | 2 |
| Luke | 8 |
| Josh | 3 |
| Juan | 12 |
| Terry | 10 |
| Lucas | 4 |
| Valentine | 6 |
| Jamal | 12 |
| Hector | 10 |
| Tony | 6 |
| Daniel | 7 |

Which score represents the median (middle) score?

_____

Explain how you decided.

_____

_____

_____

_____

_____

Test Taking Tips

How can you organize the numbers to find the median score?

**4** Jessica is greeting relatives at the airport. The schedule shows arrival times. Jessica will meet her grandmother from Miami at the gate. How much longer will they have to wait for her cousin, who is coming from Atlanta?

_____

Explain how you decided.

| Flight Arrivals | |
| --- | --- |
| Arriving From | Arrival Time |
| Atlanta | 5:35 P.M. |
| Boston | 2:10 P.M. |
| Chicago | 8:20 P.M. |
| Miami | 1:45 P.M. |

_____

_____

_____

Test Taking Tips

When will her grandmother arrive from Miami?

When will her cousin arrive from Atlanta?

How can you find the difference between those times?

Name _____

**5** Mr. Romero's class and Ms. Caldwell's class are going on a picnic. They need to pack box lunches for their classes.

Each lunch box measures
8 in. x 8 in. x 8 in.

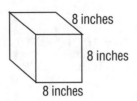

8 inches
8 inches
8 inches

They will pack the lunch boxes in a large container like the one drawn below.

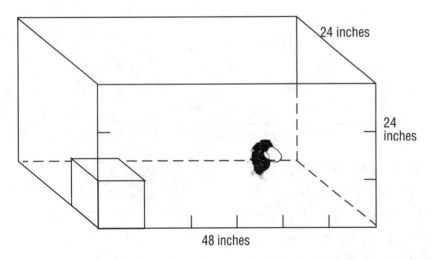

24 inches

24 inches

48 inches

How many boxes can fit in the lowest layer of the box?

_____

Draw a picture of that layer.

## Test Taking Tips

How many boxes fit in the first layer of the large container?

Name _____

**5** How many little boxes will fit in the large container?

_____

Use pictures and diagrams to help explain your thinking.

**Test Taking Tips**

How can you use a picture to understand the problem?

**1** Which of the following figures shows a right triangle inside a quadrilateral?

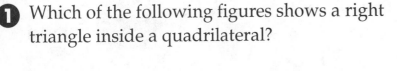

 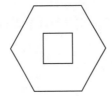

Ⓐ              Ⓑ

 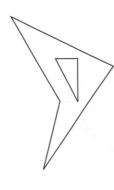

Ⓒ              Ⓓ

**Test Taking Tips**

What is always true about right triangles?

What is a quadrilateral?

---

**2** The faces of a number cube are numbered from 1 to 6.

After you toss the cube, you'll look at the number on top.

Which of the following outcomes is possible?

0     4     8     10     12

Ⓕ 0

Ⓖ 4

Ⓗ 8

Ⓘ 12

**Test Taking Tips**

How can making a list of possible outcomes help you solve the problem?

Name _____

**3** Jamal noticed a pattern in these numbers.

6, 12, 18, 24, 30,…

What would be the next three numbers in the pattern?

_____

Describe the pattern that helps you predict the next numbers.

_____

_____

_____

Test Taking Tips

How is each number related to the number that comes before it?

**4** Which graph is more likely to show the heights of a group of fourth graders?

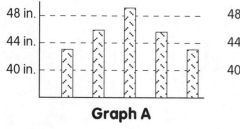 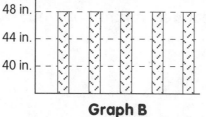

**Graph A**                    **Graph B**

Explain how you decided.

_____

_____

_____

Test Taking Tips

What do you notice about the height of students in your class?

Name _____

**5** Use the grid below. Start at the point (6, 4). Then show three more points to form a square when the points are connected.

Test Taking Tips

Solve
Long Answer
Think • Explain

How do you know where the point (6,4) is located?

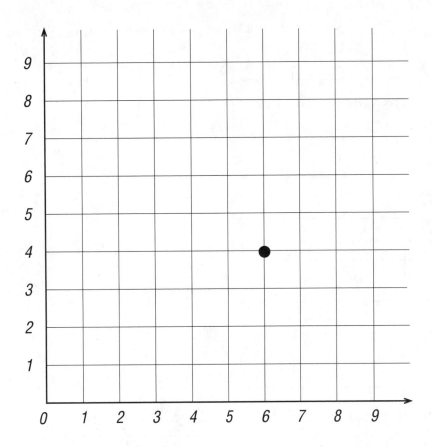

Write the ordered pair for each point on your square.

(6, 4)

_____

_____

_____

Grade 4 • Harcourt Brace School Publishers

Name _____

**5** Explain how to name ordered pairs in a grid. Use words and numbers.

**Test Taking Tips**

How can you check that your answer is clear and complete?

_____

_____

_____

_____

_____

On the lines below, explain how you know that your shape is a square.

_____

_____

_____

_____

_____

_____

New York Test Prep

Name _____

**1** Jesse harvested pints of strawberries from the garden. How many more pints did Jesse harvest in 1994 than in 1997?

How many pints of strawberries did Jesse harvest each year?

### Jesse's Strawberry Crops

| Year | |
|------|---|
| 1997 | 🍓 🍓 🍓 |
| 1996 | 🍓 🍓 🍓 🍓 |
| 1995 | 🍓 🍓 🍓 🍓 |
| 1994 | 🍓 🍓 🍓 🍓 🍓 |
| 1993 | 🍓 🍓 |

Each 🍓 = 4 pints

Ⓐ   2 pints

Ⓑ   4 pints

Ⓒ   6 pints

Ⓓ   8 pints

---

**2** Sandy won a $15,000 shopping spree to an electronics store. She bought all the items on the list.

### What Sandy Bought

| | |
|---|---|
| 2 big-screen TV sets | $2,150 each |
| 1 stereo system | $1,750 |
| 2 computer systems | $3,580 each |

How much did each TV set cost? How many did she buy?

How can rounding help you solve the problem?

ESTIMATE to the nearest $1,000 how much money Sandy has left.

Ⓕ   between $1,000 – $2,000

Ⓖ   between $2,000 – $3,000

Ⓗ   between $3,000 – $4,000

Ⓘ   between $4,000 – $5,000

Grade 4 • Harcourt Brace School Publishers

Name _____

**3** Terrell had these coins. She bought a soda for 60¢ and crackers for 65¢.

How much money does she have left over?

_____

On the lines below, explain how you decided.

_____

_____

_____

What do you need to find out first?

---

**4** A large window is made up of four square panes. The perimeter of each pane is 40 inches. There is a piece of wood 1 inch wide around each pane.

What is the perimeter of the large window?

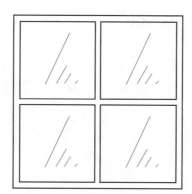

_____

_____

Remember: Perimeter is the distance around the outside edge of an object.

Test Taking Tips

How can you label parts of the picture to help solve the problem?

Name _____

**5** Joey has a new puppy. His sister, Jenna, has a big dog.

Jenna's dog weighs eight times as much as the puppy. Both pets together weigh 54 pounds.

How much does Joey's puppy weigh?

Think • Solve • Explain
Long Answer

**Test Taking Tips**

How can you make a model to show the information?

Grade 4 • Harcourt Brace School Publishers

New York Test Prep

Name _____

**5** Explain how you solved the problem.

Use words, pictures and numbers.

_____

_____

_____

_____

_____

_____

How can you check that your answer is clear and complete?

Name _____

**1** Annie went to the state fair to see the pumpkin contest. Her dad said, "The winning pumpkin weighs about four times as much as you do."

Which measure below is the most reasonable ESTIMATE of the weight of the winning pumpkin?

Ⓐ 2,000 pounds

Ⓑ 1,200 pounds

Ⓒ 300 pounds

Ⓓ 75 pounds

Test Taking Tips

How can you estimate the weight of a fourth grader?

---

**2** Use the information in the diagram below. What is the perimeter of the Sports Center building?

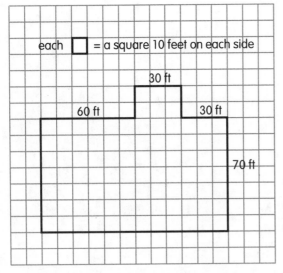

each ☐ = a square 10 feet on each side

30 ft

60 ft          30 ft

70 ft

Ⓕ 70 feet

Ⓖ 120 feet

Ⓗ 190 feet

Ⓘ 420 feet

Remember: Perimeter is the distance around a shape.

Test Taking Tips

Which measures do you need in order to solve the problem?

Grade 4 • Harcourt Brace School Publishers

Name _____

**3** Mrs. Jacoby's class and Mr. Ralston's class are going on a field trip. There are 27 students in Mrs. Jacoby's class and 31 students in Mr. Ralston's class. The two teachers and five other adults are also going. The bus can carry 65 passengers. Is there enough room on the bus?

**Test Taking Tips**

How many people are going on the field trip?

_____

On the lines below, explain how you decided.

_____

_____

_____

**4** Roberta and Salina went to the beach and drew a rectangle in the sand. Then they measured two sides using Roberta's sand shovel.

**Test Taking Tips**

How can labeling the diagram help you solve the problem?

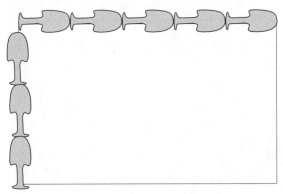

One side was 3 shovels long. Another side was 5 shovels long.

What was the perimeter of the rectangle? _____
Explain your thinking.

_____

_____

Grade 4 • Harcourt Brace School Publishers

**5** Burt has 24 feet of fencing to build a cage for his new pet rabbit. The cage can be a square or a rectangle. Use the grid paper to draw 4 different ways that Burt can build the cage using all 24 feet of fencing.

Think • Solve • Explain
Long Answer
**Test Taking Tips**

How can you check that your answer is clear and complete?

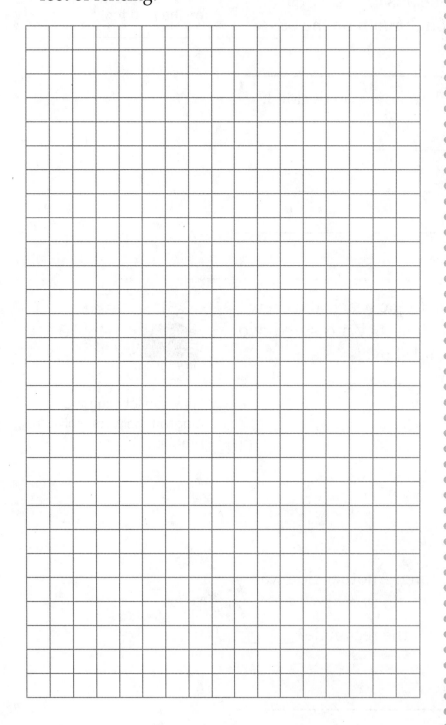

Grade 4 • Harcourt Brace School Publishers

Daily Practice
Week
16

**5** Record the length and width of each possible cage. Then check that you have used all the fencing each time. Find the area of each cage.

| Length | Width | Fence Needed (feet) | Area (square feet) |
|--------|-------|---------------------|--------------------|
|        |       |                     |                    |
|        |       |                     |                    |
|        |       |                     |                    |
|        |       |                     |                    |
|        |       |                     |                    |
|        |       |                     |                    |

What are the length and width of the cage that will give his rabbit the most room?

length: _____

width: _____

On the lines below, explain how you decided.

_____

_____

_____

_____

Test Taking Tips

How can you check that each possiblility uses all of the fencing?

**1** Alexandro went to the mall with $25 to spend. He spent $11.41 for a tee-shirt, $7.93 for a book, and $3.15 for a snack. About how much does he have left?

Ⓐ   about $10

Ⓑ   about $5

Ⓒ   about $4

Ⓓ   about $3

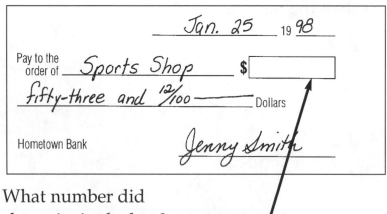

$11.41          $3.15

$7.93

**Test Taking Tips**

How can you use estimation to choose a reasonable answer?

---

**2** Billy's mom wrote a check for fifty-three dollars and twelve cents.

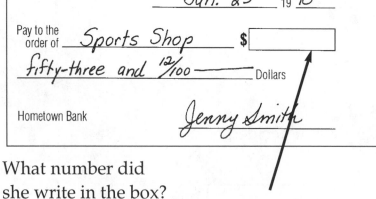

_Jan. 25_ 19 _98_

Pay to the order of _Sports Shop_   $ [          ]

_fifty-three and ¹²/₁₀₀ ———_ Dollars

Hometown Bank          _Jenny Smith_

What number did she write in the box?

Mark your answer in the grid.

Ⓕ   $53.12

Ⓖ   $53.00

Ⓗ   $35.12

Ⓘ   $5.12

**Test Taking Tips**

How can you write the words as numbers?

Grade 4 • Harcourt Brace School Publishers

**3** Georgia's class has 26 students. On Saint Patrick's Day, they had a party. Everyone either wore a green shirt or wore a green hat. Some students did both. 17 students wore a green shirt. 21 students wore green hats. How many students wearing green shirts were also wearing green hats?

Use this number line to help find the answer.

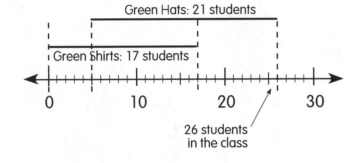

Test Taking Tips

What does the overlap of the two line segments represent?

---

**4** Write three different measurements you can use to describe a person.

_____

_____

_____

Then explain what tool you would use for each measurement.

_____

_____

_____

Test Taking Tips

What information does each kind of measurement give you?

Name _____

**5** Jodi is making cardboard cubes. Which of these patterns can she fold to make a cube?

Write OK by each net that will fold to make a cube. Write NO if it will not fold to make a cube.

Which can be folded to look like a box with a top and bottom?

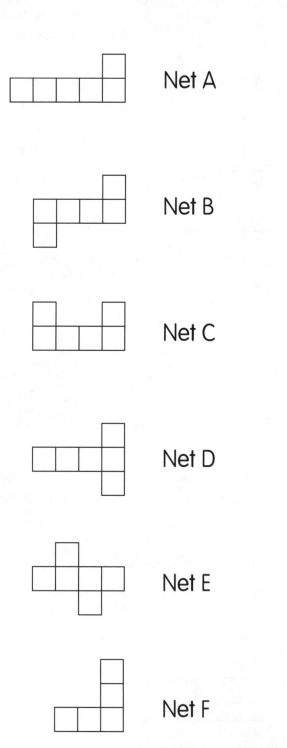

Net A

Net B

Net C

Net D

Net E

Net F

Grade 4 • Harcourt Brace School Publishers

New York Test Prep

Name _____

**5** For each net that will not be a cube, explain why it would not work.

Test
Taking
Tips

_____

_____

_____

_____

_____

_____

_____

_____

_____

_____

_____

How many faces are on a cube?

Name _____

**1** Margo put 5 dimes in an empty jar on Monday morning. Each day she added the same number of dimes as the previous day, plus two more.

How much money did she have in the jar on Friday evening?

| Monday | Tuesday | Wednesday | Thursday | Friday |
|---|---|---|---|---|
| 5 dimes<br>50¢ | | | | |

How will making a table help you record all the information you need?

- Ⓐ $1.30
- Ⓑ $3.20
- Ⓒ $4.50
- Ⓓ $45.00

**2** How many sides do eight octagons have?

- Ⓕ 16 sides
- Ⓖ 36 sides
- Ⓗ 56 sides
- Ⓘ 64 sides

What do you need to know about an octagon to solve this problem?

Grade 4 • Harcourt Brace School Publishers

New York TEST Prep

Name _____

**3** Fred works at an ice cream shop. He sells vanilla, chocolate, and strawberry ice cream. He can make double-scoop cones using one flavor or two flavors. He can make several different double-scoop cones. If he uses chocolate and vanilla, for example, he can put the chocolate on the top, or on the bottom.

How many different double-scoop cones can he make?

_____

Use pictures or diagrams to help explain your answer.

Test Taking Tips

How can you keep a record of all the combinations?

---

**4** For each gallon of gasoline Marisol's mom puts in her car, the car can travel about 26 miles. The tank holds 12 gallons.

Can Marisol's family drive 400 miles on one full tank?

_____

Explain how you decided. Use the lines below.

_____

_____

_____

Test Taking Tips

How can you use estimation to solve the problem?

Grade 4 • Harcourt Brace School Publishers

Name _____

**5** Savannah built the following three designs from tiles.

Test Taking Tips

How many tiles does she need for each design?

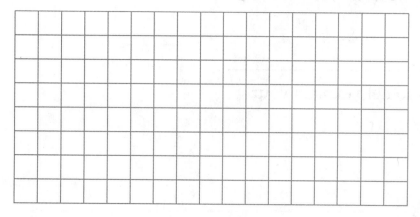

1       2       3

Follow her pattern and draw her fourth design.

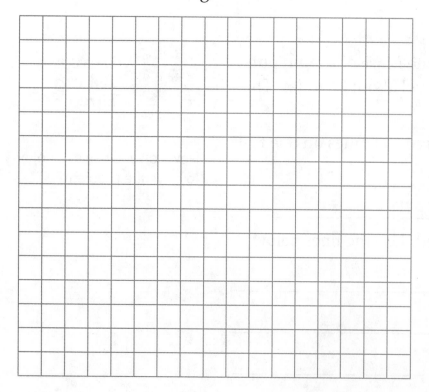

Draw her tenth design.

Grade 4 • Harcourt Brace School Publishers

Name _____

**5** What pattern is she using to make each design?

_____

_____

_____

Explain in words and drawings.

_____

_____

_____

How can you check that your answer is correct and that your explanation is clear?

**1** There are one hundred Lego® blocks in Kurt's container. The table shows the number of each block color. What percent of the legos are red?

| Color | Number of Legos |
| --- | --- |
| Red | 30 |
| Yellow | 15 |
| Blue | 40 |
| Green | 15 |
| Total | 100 |

Ⓐ  10%

Ⓑ  12%

Ⓒ  30%

Ⓓ  70%

Test
Taking
Tips

What do you need to find first to solve the problem?

**2** Mrs. Jones is thinking of a mystery number. She calls the number *m*. Starting with *m*, she adds 4. Then she multiplies her answer by 5. Next, she divides her new answer by 3. Then she subtracts 8. Her final answer is 7. What is her mystery number?

Ⓕ  5

Ⓖ  9

Ⓗ  15

Ⓘ  21

Test
Taking
Tips

How can working backward help you solve the problem?

Grade 4 • Harcourt Brace School Publishers

Name _____

**3** Lucas took 5 spelling tests this grading period. He used a calculator to average his scores.

Test #1    91

Test #2    85

Test #3    94

Test #4    92

Test #5    88

Is his solution reasonable?

_____

Explain how you decided.

_____

_____

Test Taking Tips

How do you find an average?

**4** Rachel is on a swim team. She practices five days a week. The pool is 25 meters long. She swims 50 lengths at each practice. How many meters does she swim each week?

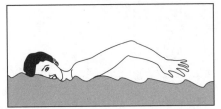

_____

Show how you found out.

_____

_____

_____

Test Taking Tips

What operation can you use to solve the problem?

Name _____

**5** Mr. Boromeo is planting a rectangular garden. He wants it to have an area of EXACTLY 48 square feet.

Draw three different rectangles that have an area of 48 square feet.

How does drawing a diagram for each rectangle help you know that the rectangles have an area of 48 square feet?

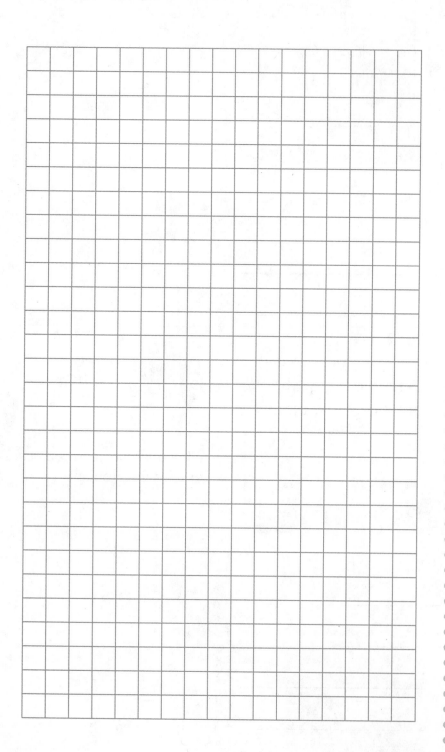

Grade 4 • Harcourt Brace School Publishers

New York Test Prep

Name _____

**5** Make a table. Show the length and width of each rectangle that you found.

**Test Taking Tips**

How can making a table help you solve this problem?

| Length | Width | Fence Needed (feet) | Area (square feet) |
|--------|-------|---------------------|--------------------|
|        |       |                     |                    |
|        |       |                     |                    |
|        |       |                     |                    |

What is the least amount of fencing he can use to enclose a rectangle with an area of 48 square feet?

_____

Use words and pictures to explain your answer.

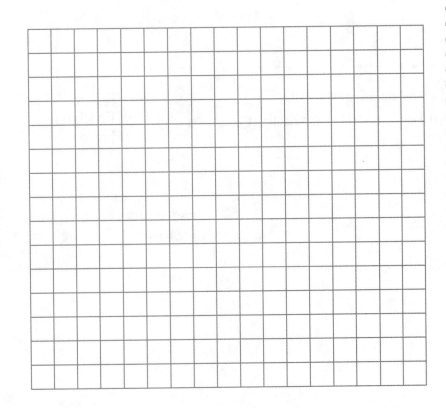

Name _____

**1** Richard drew this design.

Then he folded his paper on the dotted line and traced the design. When he unfolds the paper, what does the tracing look like?

   Ⓐ         Ⓑ         Ⓒ         Ⓓ

Where will the triangle be in the tracing?

---

**2** In Mrs. Martin's class there are 14 girls and 12 boys. What is the ratio of boys to all the students in Mrs. Martin's class?

   Ⓐ   12:14

   Ⓑ   14:12

   Ⓒ   12:26

   Ⓓ   14:26

What information do you need in order to solve the problem?

Grade 4 • Harcourt Brace School Publishers

Name _____

**3** Six friends are on a tennis team. Each player will play each of the other players only once. How many tennis games will they play?

Show how you solved the problem. Explain your thinking.

Solve
Think
Explain
Short
Answer
Test
Taking
Tips

How can a chart or picture help you solve the problem?

_____

_____

_____

_____

**4** Leo has a sister, Melanie. Melanie is twice as old as Leo. If you add their ages together you get 27.

How old is Leo? _____

How old is Melanie? _____

Show your work or explain how you solved the problem.

Solve
Think
Explain
Short
Answer
Test
Taking
Tips

How can you use a model to solve the problem?

_____

_____

_____

_____

Grade 4 • Harcourt Brace School Publishers

Name _____

**5** Samuel saw a bus full of children bringing their dogs to a dog show. He counted 42 legs in all. How many children and how many dogs could be on the bus?

Write some guesses in the chart. You may find more than one correct answer!

**Test Taking Tips**

How can you use guess and check to solve the problem?

Why should you guess fewer than 21 children?

| Children | | Dogs | | Total: Children + Dogs | |
|---|---|---|---|---|---|
| How many children? | How many legs? | How many dogs? | How many legs? | How many legs total? | Comments |
| | | | | | |
| | | | | | |
| | | | | | |
| | | | | | |
| | | | | | |
| | | | | | |

Grade 4 • Harcourt Brace School Publishers

**5** What did you learn by studying your guess and check chart? Explain your thinking on the lines below.

_____

_____

_____

_____

Test Taking Tips

How can you check that your answer is clear and complete?

Name _____

**1** Raoul likes to keep a weather watch. One February morning, the temperature was 4° C. Later that day, the temperature rose to 23° C.

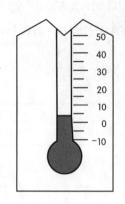

How many degrees Celsius did the temperature rise?

Ⓐ 4°C

Ⓑ 19°C

Ⓒ 23°C

Ⓓ 27°C

**Test Taking Tips**

How can using the scale on the thermometer help you solve the problem?

**2** Three people drove together to Tennessee. Murray drove five hours. Malcolm drove three hours, and Xavier drove two hours. They averaged sixty miles per hour.

How many miles did they travel?

Ⓕ 300 miles

Ⓖ 480 miles

Ⓗ 600 miles

Ⓘ 1,800 miles

**Test Taking Tips**

How many hours did their trip last?

How will this information help you solve the problem?

**84**

New York Test Prep

Grade 4 • Harcourt Brace School Publishers

Name _____

**3** On Michael's basketball team, the height of each player's jump is measured in inches. Each player's best jump is shown in the chart.

| How High Can You Jump? | |
|---|---|
| Michael | 42 inches |
| Patrick | 27 inches |
| Charles | 37 inches |
| Angelo | 31 inches |
| Taoran | 40 inches |

What is the **median** of the players' best jumps?

_____

Explain how to find the median.

_____

_____

Think • Solve • Explain
Short Answer
**Test Taking Tips**

How can you organize the numbers to help you find the median?

**4** Kendra made this design with pattern blocks.

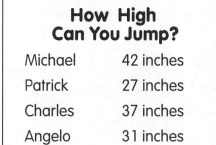

20 points

1 point

5 points

2 points

How many points is her design worth? Explain how you found your answer.

_____

_____

Think • Solve • Explain
Short Answer
**Test Taking Tips**

How many points is each shape worth?

How many of each shape did she use?

Think • Solve • Explain — Long Answer

**Test Taking Tips**

**5** Jodi is buying supplies to start a window garden. She has $5 to spend.

How does rounding decimals to the nearest tenth help solve the problem?

One bag of soil fills 3 clay pots.

Make a shopping list of the items she can buy on her trip to the garden center. Round the prices shown on the tags to the nearest 10 cents and include rounded prices for the items on your shopping list.

_____

_____

_____

_____

_____

_____

**86**

Grade 4 • Harcourt Brace School Publishers

**5** She wants to have 5 clay pots full of plants. Can she afford to buy 5 clay pots, enough soil for the pots, and seeds?

_____

Remember, one bag of soil fills 3 clay pots.

Explain on the lines below.

_____

_____

_____

_____

_____

How can you check that your answer is clear and complete?

Name _____

**1** Which of the following is NOT equal to 3?

Ⓐ  3.00

Ⓑ  12 ÷ 4

Ⓒ  $\frac{3}{9}$

Ⓓ  1 × 3

Test Taking Tips

How does thinking about equivalent forms of a number help you solve the problem?

---

**2** Leah and her brother are saving to buy a computer game that costs $49.95. They saved dimes in their piggy bank. They put the dimes into four rolls. Each roll holds 50 dimes.

How many more rolls of dimes do they need in order to buy the computer game?

Ⓕ  4 more rolls

Ⓖ  5 more rolls

Ⓗ  6 more rolls

Ⓘ  7 more rolls

Test Taking Tips

What do you need to find out first?

Grade 4 • Harcourt Brace School Publishers

Name _____

**3** Mr. Clark's class conducted an experiment to see how many raisins there are in a snack-size box. One group made this graph of their data:

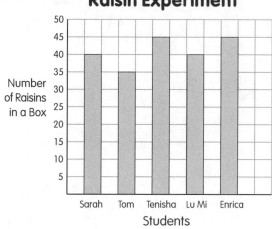

**Raisin Experiment**

What is the AVERAGE number of raisins per box? _____

Show how you solved the problem.

_____

_____

What clues about the average number of raisins in a box can you get from the bars on the bar graph?

**4** What is the probability of spinning a lion?

_____

Explain how you decided.

_____

_____

_____

What are the possible outcomes?

What fractional part of the spinner shows a lion?

 Grade 4 • Harcourt Brace School Publishers

New York Test Prep

Name _____

**5** Alice spent $28 on new notebooks and organizer pockets. Notebooks cost $3 and organizer pockets cost $2. Alice bought 12 items.

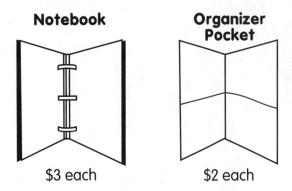

**Notebook**
$3 each

**Organizer Pocket**
$2 each

How many of each did she buy?

Use the chart to record your guesses.

|  | Notebooks ($3 each) | | Organizer Pockets ($2 each) | | Total Expense |
|---|---|---|---|---|---|
|  | How many? | How much money? | How many? | How much money? | Notebooks + Organizers |
| Guess #1 |  |  |  |  |  |
| Guess #2 |  |  |  |  |  |
| Guess #3 |  |  |  |  |  |
| Guess #4 |  |  |  |  |  |
| Guess #5 |  |  |  |  |  |
| Guess #6 |  |  |  |  |  |

Think • Solve • Explain
Long Answer

**Test Taking Tips**

How will using guess and check help you solve the problem?

Grade 4 • Harcourt Brace School Publishers

Name _____

**5** How many of each did she buy?

_____

Explain how you can learn from a wrong guess to make a better one the next time.

_____

_____

_____

_____

_____

**Test Taking Tips**

How can you check that your answer is clear and complete?

Name _____

**1** Sam said, "We ate five sixths of the pizza." Which picture can be used to show the amount of pizza left?

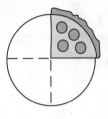
Ⓐ

Ⓑ

Ⓒ

Ⓓ

**Test Taking Tips**

How many slices could have been in the pizza?

---

**2** In music class there are four more boys than girls. If there are 28 students in all, how many are boys?

Ⓕ 14

Ⓖ 16

Ⓗ 18

Ⓘ 20

**Test Taking Tips**

How can you use guess and check to solve the problem?

Name _____

**3** Circle the polygons.

A          B          C

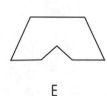

D          E

Explain how you know.

_____

_____

_____

Test
Taking
Tips

What math word do you
need to know to solve the
problem?

---

**4** Jasmin's kindergarten class has three boxes of
crayons at each activity table in the classroom.
There are four activity tables.

Half of the boxes hold 15 crayons each. The rest
hold 20 crayons each. How many crayons are in
the classroom?

Explain how you found out.

_____

_____

_____

Test
Taking
Tips

What do you need to figure
out first?

Grade 4 • Harcourt Brace School Publishers

Name _____

**5** Kim, Cathy, and Jenny drove together to Florida for a vacation. Kim drove for 3 hours. Cathy drove for 5 hours. Jenny drove the rest of the time.

Together, Kim and Cathy drove twice as many hours as Jenny. How many hours did Jenny drive? Draw a diagram to help solve the problem.

How can you draw a picture or make a diagram to show the information?

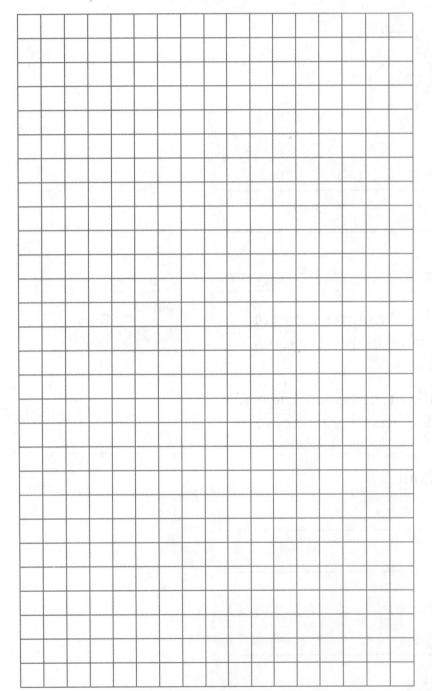

Name _____

**5** How long did Jenny drive?

_____

Explain how you solved the problem. Use
pictures, numbers, and words.

_____

_____

_____

_____

**Test Taking Tips**

How can you use what you
know about fractions to help
solve the problem?

How can you check to see if
your answer is right?

Name _____

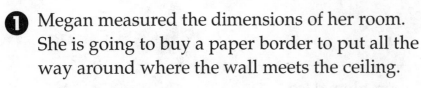
**1** Megan measured the dimensions of her room. She is going to buy a paper border to put all the way around where the wall meets the ceiling.

Which could she use to find out how much border to buy?

10 ft

**Megan's Room**

9 ft

Ⓐ 9 ft x 10 ft

Ⓑ 9 ft + 10 ft

Ⓒ 10 ft ÷ 9 ft

Ⓓ 9 ft + 10 ft + 9 ft + 10 ft

**Test Taking Tips**

How can you use the information in the diagram to help you choose the correct answer?

**2** Jana noticed that the temperature at 4 P.M. was 65 °F. During the night, the temperature was 50 °F.

How many degrees did the temperature drop?

Ⓕ 5

Ⓖ 10

Ⓗ 15

Ⓘ 25

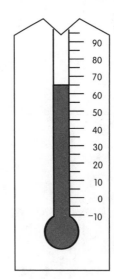

**Test Taking Tips**

How can you use the scale on the thermometer to solve the problem?

Grade 4 • Harcourt Brace School Publishers

Name _____

**3** Timmy's family spent the weekend at the beach. Timmy recorded the temperature each day at noon. On Friday, the temperature was 78° F. On Saturday, it was 82° F. On Sunday, the temperature was 83° F.

What was the average noon temperature?

_____

Explain how you found your answer.

_____

_____

_____

_____

**Test Taking Tips**

How do you find an average?

---

**4** Ms. Schultz's class conducted a survey to find out which hand students use to write. Here are their results.

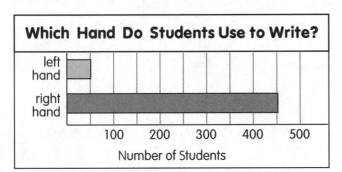

**Which Hand Do Students Use to Write?**

left hand

right hand

100   200   300   400   500
Number of Students

What fraction of the people surveyed are left-handed? _____

Explain how you decided.

_____

_____

**Test Taking Tips**

How many students were surveyed?

How many of the surveyed students are left-handed?

Grade 4 • Harcourt Brace School Publishers

Name _____

**5** The students in Mrs. Hunter's class are making their own trail mix for a hiking trip. Each bag will contain exactly 12 ounces of mix.

Each mix must contain three or more ingredients. Use the chart to show 3 different trail mixes the students could make.

Test Taking Tips

Why can't you put 12 ounces of peanuts in a mix?

| Ingredient | Mix #1 | Mix #2 | Mix #3 |
|---|---|---|---|
| peanuts | | | |
| chocolate chips | | | |
| sunflower seeds | | | |
| raisins | | | |
| banana chips | | | |
| date pieces | | | |
| other: | | | |
| **TOTAL AMOUNT** | 12 ounces | 12 ounces | 12 ounces |

Grade 4 • Harcourt Brace School Publishers

New York Test Prep

**5** The students are making a special bag of trail mix for Mrs. Hunter, the teacher who will take them hiking. This mix will have 5 ingredients and weigh one pound, or 16 ounces.

Use the ingredients listed on page 98 to make a one-pound mix for the teacher.

Use the ingredients listed on page 98

**Test Taking Tips**

Why can't you put 4 oz of each ingredient in this mix for the teacher?

| Ingredient | Amount in Ounces |
|---|---|
| #1 | |
| #2 | |
| #3 | |
| #4 | |
| #5 | |
| **TOTAL AMOUNT** | |

Name _____

**1** Jeff went to the store to buy ten bottles of water.

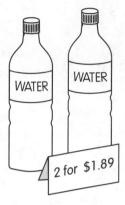

2 for $1.89

About how much did he pay?

Ⓐ about $2

Ⓑ about $10

Ⓒ about $19

Ⓓ about $22

**Test Taking Tips**

How can you use estimation to choose a reasonable answer?

**2** The track team finished a race. The runners recorded their times.

| Tim  | 23.03 seconds |
| Bill | 23.30 seconds |
| Joe  | 23.27 seconds |
| Pete | 23.72 seconds |

Which time was the fastest?

Ⓕ 23.03

Ⓖ 23.27

Ⓗ 23.30

Ⓘ 23.72

**Test Taking Tips**

How can ordering the decimals from least to greatest help you solve the problem?

Grade 4 • Harcourt Brace School Publishers

**3** Jon and Alexis are sharing a bowl of pretzels. Jon ate $\frac{3}{10}$ of the pretzels. Alexis ate 0.20 of the pretzels.

Who ate more pretzels?

_____

Explain how you decided. Write an expression using < or >.

_____

_____

_____

_____

How does writing an equivalent decimal for the fraction help you solve the problem?

**4** Maria likes to go far on inline skates. She skated 1 kilometer her first week. Each week, she skated 1 more kilometer than the week before. She did this for 7 weeks.

What was the total number of kilometers she skated?

_____

How can you organize the information into a table to find the total?

Grade 4 • Harcourt Brace School Publishers

Name _____

**5** In the 1996 Olympic Games in Atlanta, Georgia, the United States and Germany had the fastest times in the Women's Swimming Relay.

How many seconds are in a minute?

How can you find the total time for the U.S. team?

Germany's team of four swimmers finished in 3 minutes, 57 seconds.

Here are the times for swimmers on the U.S. team:

| | |
|---|---|
| 1st swimmer | 48.20 seconds |
| 2nd swimmer | 48.36 seconds |
| 3rd swimmer | 49.46 seconds |
| 4th swimmer | 47.98 seconds |

Which team was faster? _____

By how many seconds? _____

Grade 4 • Harcourt Brace School Publishers

Name _____

**5** Write step-by-step directions to explain how to solve the problem.

_____

_____

_____

_____

_____

_____

Did you write clear directions so that someone else could solve the problem in the same way?

Name _____

**1** Which are the names of the faces on this three-dimensional figure?

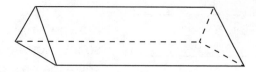

Ⓐ triangles and squares

Ⓑ rectangles and squares

Ⓒ triangles and hexagons

Ⓓ triangles and rectangles

Test Taking Tips

What math words do you need to know to solve the problem?

**2** Marvella and her dad were making a swing. They bought two lengths of heavy rope that were each 3.5 meters long. The rope cost $3.29 per meter. How much did they pay for the rope?

Ⓕ $6.58

Ⓖ $11.51

Ⓗ $21.56

Ⓘ $23.03

Test Taking Tips

How much rope did they buy?

**3** Colin's stepfather is making a new board for Colin's electric train village.

What is the perimeter of Colin's train board?

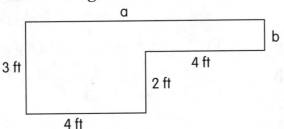

a

b

3 ft

4 ft

2 ft

4 ft

_____

Remember: Perimeter is the distance around a shape.

Explain how you decided.

_____

_____

Test Taking Tips

Short Answer

How can you use the drawing to find the missing measures?

---

**4** Lloyd has a coupon worth $1.00 to spend at a store. He will have to pay the sales tax in cash.

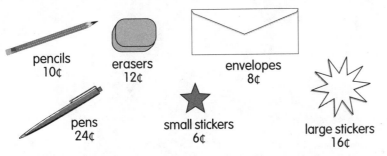

pencils
10¢

erasers
12¢

envelopes
8¢

pens
24¢

small stickers
6¢

large stickers
16¢

What can Lloyd buy that will use up his coupon? Make a table to show two different ways he can use the whole coupon.

Test Taking Tips

Short Answer

How will you set up your table to help solve the problem?

You can write 10¢ as $0.10. How will writing all the prices of the items with a dollar sign and decimal help you know when you have spent $1.00?

Name _____

**5** Sasha's class put a rain gauge outside their classroom for five months. They collected the following information:

| September | 7 inches of rain |
| October | 8 inches of rain |
| November | 7 inches of rain |
| December | 3 inches of rain |
| January | 2 inches of rain |

Use this information to make a bar graph.

Check to see that your graph has

- a title
- an appropriate scale
- label for each bar
- accurate data

What scale can you use for your bar graph?

Grade 4 • Harcourt Brace School Publishers

Name _____

**5**

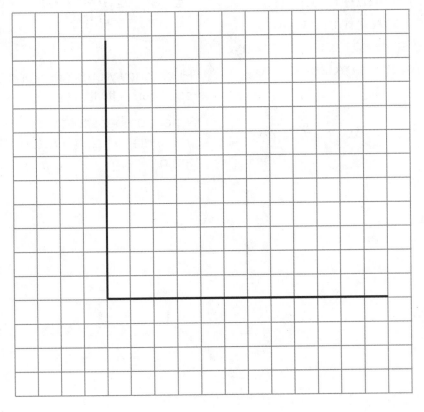

How much rainfall will be represented by each line on your graph?

Write a question you can answer using the information in the graph.

_____

_____

_____

_____

Grade 4 • Harcourt Brace School Publishers

Name _____

**1** Alana entered the county spelling bee. She spelled 47 words correctly before she made a mistake. If she had spelled three more words correctly, she would have spelled twice as many words as last year. How many words did she spell correctly last year?

Ⓐ  25

Ⓑ  27

Ⓒ  32

Ⓓ  35

**Test Taking Tips**

How many words did Alana spell correctly this year?

What number sentence can you write to help you solve the problem?

**2** Michelle and Heather are measuring the volume of a new aquarium for their classroom. Michelle poured in 83 cups of water. Heather poured in 77 cups.

How many QUARTS of water did the girls put into the aquarium?

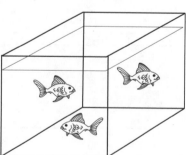

Remember, 4 cups = 1 quart

Ⓕ  19 quarts

Ⓖ  20 quarts

Ⓗ  31 quarts

Ⓘ  40 quarts

**Test Taking Tips**

How can you change cups to quarts?

Grade 4 • Harcourt Brace School Publishers

Name _____

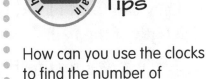
**3** The music teacher at school is encouraging children to practice playing their instruments.

Sauri, Thomas, and Dan each begin practicing at 7 o'clock.

Sauri practiced half an hour a day for 5 days.

Thomas practiced one third of an hour a day for 10 days.

Dan practiced one fourth of an hour a day for 12 days.

Who spent the most time practicing? _____

Explain how you found your answer.

_____

_____

Test Taking Tips

How can you use the clocks to find the number of minutes in each fraction of an hour?

**4** Angelo and Justin were painting a mural. Justin needed $\frac{2}{6}$ cup of purple paint. "Just put in $\frac{1}{3}$ cup of blue paint and $\frac{1}{3}$ cup of red paint. That will give you exactly $\frac{2}{6}$ cup of purple paint," Angelo said.

Do you think Angelo is right? _____

Explain your thinking.

_____

_____

_____

Test Taking Tips

What is the correct way to add fractions?

Grade 4 • Harcourt Brace School Publishers

Name _____

**5** Benjie is helping his little sister build with blocks. The blue blocks are all the same length. They can fit 24 blocks end to end down the length of the hall.

Benjie measures one blue block and finds that it is 6 inches long.

How long is the hallway?

_____ inches

_____ feet

_____ yards

Use pictures or diagrams to help explain your thinking.

Test Taking Tips

How many inches are in one foot?

How many feet are in one yard?

Daily Practice
Week
27

**5** Benjie got some new large blocks for his birthday. Each block is 2 feet long.

How many of these blocks will fit in the hall placed end to end? _____

Draw a picture and use numbers to explain.

When you change feet to yards, will you have fewer or more yards than feet?

**1** Janet is putting away her little brother's blocks. There are 48 blocks in all. She wants to put them on a shelf with the same number of blocks in each layer. Which of the following is NOT a possible way to arrange the blocks?

Ⓐ 4 wide, 4 high, and 3 deep

Ⓑ 12 wide, 2 high and 2 deep

Ⓒ 16 wide, 1 high and 3 deep

Ⓓ 9 wide, 2 high and 2 deep

**Test Taking Tips**

How many blocks are in each answer choice?

**2** The sign in the elevator shows that it cannot carry more than 2,000 pounds. Twelve people are waiting for the elevator. Their average weight is 160 pounds. How many more pounds can the elevator carry?

Ⓕ 80 lb more

Ⓖ 400 lb more

Ⓗ 1,520 lb more

Ⓘ 1,840 lb more

**Test Taking Tips**

What do you need to find first?

Grade 4 • Harcourt Brace School Publishers

Name _____

**3** Paula surveyed the girls in her school. One third of the girls are wearing shirts with buttons and half of the girls are wearing tee-shirts. The rest of the girls are wearing dresses.

Are there more girls wearing shirts with buttons or tee-shirts?

Explain how you decided.

_____

_____

_____

_____

**Think • Solve • Explain**
Short Answer
**Test Taking Tips**

How can you compare the two fractions?

---

**4** Tony's aunt served pizza for his birthday party. Each person at the party ate two pieces of pizza. All the pieces were the same size. Here is what was left at the end of the party.

How many people were at the party?

Explain your thinking.

_____

_____

_____

**Think • Solve • Explain**
Short Answer
**Test Taking Tips**

What information is given in the picture?

**5** LaShondra is helping her brother make a float at the football parade. They are making a model of a rocket because the team is called the Elm Street School Rockets. This is what they want their rocket to look like.

How can you use the pattern for the rocket to help solve the problem?

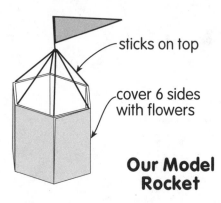

sticks on top

cover 6 sides with flowers

**Our Model Rocket**

They have made this pattern for the cardboard pieces they need for the rocket.

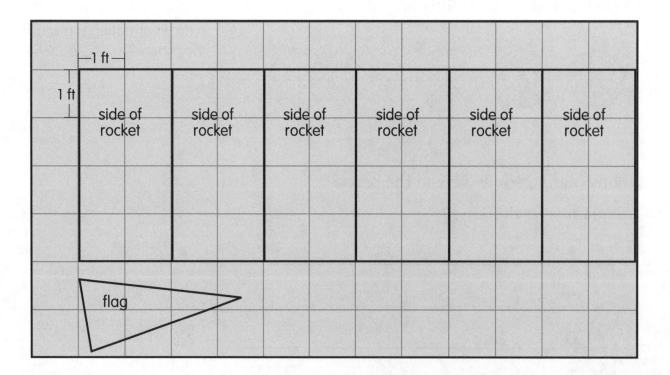

Grade 4 • Harcourt Brace School Publishers

**Test Taking Tips**

**5** Find the area of one side of the rocket. How many square feet?

_____

Find the total area of all the rocket sides. How many square feet?

_____

Estimate the area of the flag. How many square feet?

_____

How much cardboard will be left over after they cut out the rocket and flag?

_____

Explain how you found the area of the rocket, the flag, and the extra cardboard.

_____

_____

_____

_____

How can you check to see if your answers are right?

Name _____

**1**
Which shape is Jorge least likely to spin?

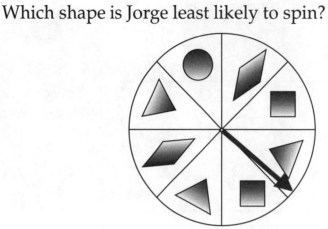

Ⓐ

Ⓑ

Ⓒ

Ⓓ

**2**
Megan glued a lace border around a picture of her cat. How much lace did she need?

20 inches

Which expression can you use to solve the problem?

15 inches

Ⓕ  15 × 20

Ⓖ  20 × 20

Ⓗ  20 + 15

Ⓘ  15 + 20 + 15 + 20

**3** Which tool should Glenn use to measure the milk that he needs to make the pancakes in the recipe?

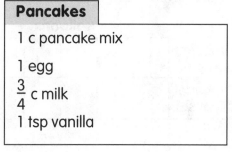

**Pancakes**

1 c pancake mix

1 egg

$\frac{3}{4}$ c milk

1 tsp vanilla

Ⓐ

Ⓑ

Ⓒ

Ⓓ

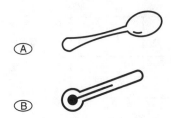

**4** Sandor's mother bought him a shirt for $29.50 and a jacket for $60. She paid with a $100 bill. How much change should she receive?

Ⓕ  $10.50

Ⓖ  $11.50

Ⓗ  $31.50

Ⓘ  $40.00

**5** Janie wants to buy balloons. The ones she wants come in packages of eight. How many packages should she buy if she needs 48 balloons?

**Balloons**

| Number of Packages | 1 | 2 | 3 | 4 | 5 | 6 | 7 | 8 |
|---|---|---|---|---|---|---|---|---|
| Number of Balloons | 8 | 16 | | | | | | |

- Ⓐ   5 packages

- Ⓑ   6 packages

- Ⓒ   7 packages

- Ⓓ   8 packages

**6** Nick's aunt brought five trays of muffins to the bake sale. Each tray had nine muffins. By noon, they had sold 20 muffins. How many muffins were left to sell?

- Ⓕ   11 muffins

- Ⓖ   15 muffins

- Ⓗ   20 muffins

- Ⓘ   25 muffins

Grade 4 • Harcourt Brace School Publishers

Name _____

**7** Which figures have a line of symmetry?
Write yes or no below each figure.
Then draw the line of symmetry if there is one.

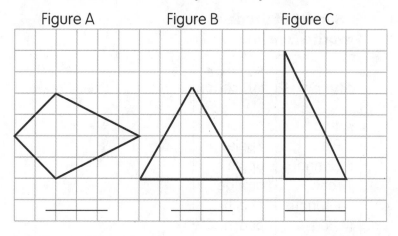

Figure A          Figure B          Figure C

On the lines below, explain how you decided.

_____

_____

**8** Anna wants to buy a set of pastels for her art
projects. The pastels cost $49.95 plus tax. Anna has
saved $3 each week for seven weeks. How much has
she saved?

Write a number sentence and solve. Then explain
how you know your answer is correct.

_____

_____

_____

_____

_____

_____

**9** Miss Jones's fourth-grade class took a survey of students' favorite lunch box fruit. The results are shown in the list below.

**Survey of Student Favorite Lunchbox Fruit**

| Student | Favorite Lunchbox Fruit |
|---------|-------------------------|
| Arturo | banana |
| Li Ping | apple |
| Susanna | apple |
| Tyrone | orange |
| Shalvindra | peach |
| Myron | peach |
| Janine | peach |
| Sherell | orange |
| Megan | banana |
| Nick | apple |
| Simon | apple |
| Stephanie | apple |
| Daesun | orange |
| Beth | raisins |
| Jon | orange |
| Willie | apple |
| Anna | apple |
| Marison | banana |
| Taleah | apple |
| Charles | raisins |

Complete a table that shows the data.

**Favorite Lunchbox Fruit**

| Fruit | Votes by Tally | Number |
|-------|----------------|--------|
| Banana | | |
| Apple | | |
| Orange | | |
| Peach | | |
| Raisins | | |

Name _____

**9** In the grid below, make a bar graph to show the results of the survey. Be sure that your graph has

a title

a label for each bar

a scale

accurate information

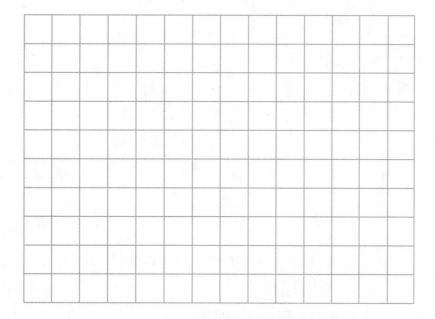

On the lines below, write one conclusion about Favorite Lunchbox Fruits. Explain how the graph supports your conclusion.

_____

_____

_____

_____

_____

_____

Grade 4 • Harcourt Brace School Publishers

Name _____

**10** Which pair of figures is the same size and shape?

Ⓐ
Ⓑ
Ⓒ
Ⓓ

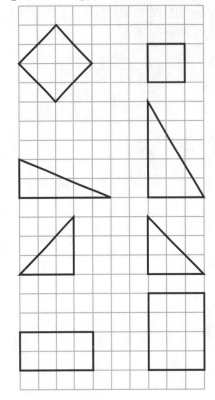

**11** Mrs. Chin's class took a survey. The results are shown in the graph below.

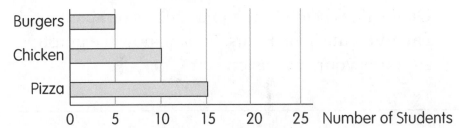

Favorite Take-Out Food

Which statement is NOT supported by the graph?

Ⓕ Fifteen people prefer pizza.

Ⓖ More people prefer chicken to burgers.

Ⓗ Five out of 30 people prefer burgers.

Ⓘ Most girls voted for pizza.

Grade 4 • Harcourt Brace School Publishers

Name _____

**12** Tallie needs $\frac{3}{4}$ cup sugar to make a cake. Which picture shows the amount of sugar she needs?

Ⓐ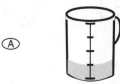

Ⓑ

Ⓒ

Ⓓ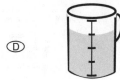

**13** What temperature is shown on the thermometer?

Ⓕ 100°

Ⓖ 75°

Ⓗ 72°

Ⓘ 70°

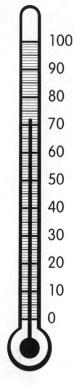

**14**  Myra, Tricia, Eleanor, and Rusty formed a reading club. On Saturday, Myra read from 3:00 P.M. to 4:00 P.M. Tricia read from 3:00 P.M.to 3:45 P.M.. Eleanor read from 3:00 P.M.to 4:10 P.M.. Rusty read from 3:00 P.M.to 3:35 P.M.. How many minutes did they read in all?

Remember: 1 hour = 60 minutes

Ⓐ 195 minutes

Ⓑ 200 minutes

Ⓒ 210 minutes

Ⓓ 235 minutes

**15**  Rachel's brother said, "I have three thousand, nine hundred seven baseball cards in my collection." Write the number of cards in his collection in standard form.

Ⓕ 3,097

Ⓖ 3,907

Ⓗ 3,970

Ⓘ 3,977

Name _____

## Notes

Problems that I answered correctly.

_____

_____

_____

_____

_____

_____

_____

Problems that I did not understand.

_____

_____

_____

_____

_____

Vocabulary that I need to learn.

_____

_____

_____

_____

**1**

The fourth graders took a pet survey. The pictograph shows the number of students by class in the fourth grade who own pets. Which class has the most students who own pets?

**Who Owns Pets?**

| Class | Number of Students |
|-------|--------------------|
| Mrs. Jenson | 🐱 🐱 🐱 |
| Mr. Chen | 🐱 🐱 |
| Ms. Clarke | 🐱 🐱 🐱 🐱 |
| Ms. Morales | 🐱 🐱 🐱 🐱 |

Key: 🐱 = 5 students.

Ⓐ Mrs. Jenson

Ⓑ Mr. Chen

Ⓒ Ms. Clarke

Ⓓ Ms. Morales

**2**

LaToya and James each have some marbles. They keep them in jars. Compare the number of marbles that James and LaToya have. Which expression below shows the comparison of James's marbles to LaToya's marbles?

Ⓕ 6 > 9

Ⓖ 9 < 6

Ⓗ 9 = 6

Ⓘ 6 < 9

**LaToya's Jar**

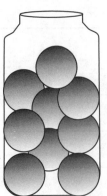

**James's Jar**

**3**

Akhmed recorded the temperature outside his house at noon each day from August 10 to August 20. On which days was the temperature below 80°?

Ⓐ   August 11,12, and 13

Ⓑ   August 13, 15, and 16

Ⓒ   August 13, 16, and 19

Ⓓ   August 15, 16, and 17

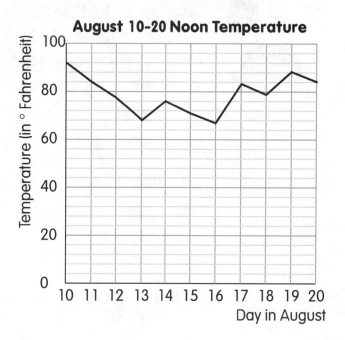

**4**

Greg is adding beans to a jar by small scoops. Look at the pictures below showing the jar after each scoop.

If Greg keeps adding beans by the scoop, how many beans will there be after the fifth scoop?

Ⓕ   20

Ⓖ   22

Ⓗ   24

Ⓘ   25

**Greg's Jar**

  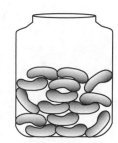

After 1st scoop    After 2nd scoop    After 3rd scoop

Name _____

**5**

Shaylan and Allison are collecting buttons. They have one thousand, three hundred seventy-four buttons. How many buttons are in their collection? Write the number using digits.

Ⓐ 1,374

Ⓑ 1,734

Ⓒ 10,374

Ⓓ 13,740

**6**

Aaron arranged a tray of cookies to take to his grandmother. He made four rows of cookies. He put 12 cookies in each row. How many cookies did he take to his grandmother?

Ⓕ 12

Ⓖ 24

Ⓗ 48

Ⓘ 60

Grade 4 • Harcourt Brace School Publishers

**7**

Joey and his dad went on a five-day camping trip. They wanted to fill up a jar with interesting pebbles to put in their turtle's aquarium. The picture shows how many pebbles they collected the first day. ESTIMATE how many days it will take to fill the jar if they collect about the same number every day. On the lines below, explain your estimation strategy.

**Joey's Jar**

After 1st day

_____

_____

_____

**8**

Sabrina drew the following picture for her friend, Andrew. She asked him to find all the squares he could. How many can you find? On the lines below, tell how many squares you found and write how you know you have found them all.

_____

_____

_____

_____

_____

_____

Name _____

**9**

The McCoys are making plans to build a house. They have a lot that measures 60 feet wide and 100 feet deep.

They have made a drawing of the house they want to build.

**The McCoys' Property and House Plan**

60 feet

Grass

House

100 feet

Garage

10 feet | Driveway

Street

10 feet

Grade 4 • Harcourt Brace School Publishers

Name _____

**9** Find the area of the house in square feet.

_____

_____

_____

_____

Find the area of the garage and the driveway in square feet.

_____

_____

_____

_____

The McCoys will plant grass from the front wall of their house to the back of the lot. How many square feet of grass will they plant?

On the lines below, explain how you solved the problem.

_____

_____

_____

_____

_____

_____

Name _____

**10** Darlene's class took a survey. They counted the buttons they were wearing. The list shows their findings. What is the mode of the data?

Remember: The mode is the number that is listed most often in a set of data.

Ⓐ 1

Ⓑ 3

Ⓒ 4

Ⓓ 6

**How Many Buttons Do We Have?**

| Student | Number of Buttons |
|---------|-------------------|
| Darlene | 4 |
| Sarah | 5 |
| Micah | 1 |
| Sander | 0 |
| Terry | 4 |
| Henry | 3 |
| Jamal | 1 |
| Thomas | 4 |
| Jared | 4 |
| Shelly | 6 |

**11** What is the area of the square in Tracy's design?

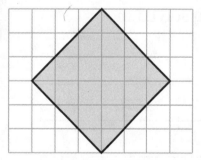

Ⓕ 12 square units

Ⓖ 14 square units

Ⓗ 16 square units

Ⓘ 18 square units

**12**

Shirin made a map of her neighborhood on a grid.

Which ordered pair names the location of the school?

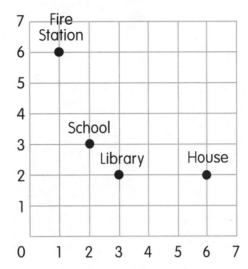

Ⓐ  (2, 3)

Ⓑ  (1, 6)

Ⓒ  (6, 2)

Ⓓ  (3, 2)

**13**

A fourth grader should get about 9 hours of sleep every night. How many hours should a fourth grader sleep every week?

Ⓕ  36 hours

Ⓖ  45 hours

Ⓗ  63 hours

Ⓘ  72 hours

Name _____

**14**  Cliff made a pattern of numbers.

1, 2, 4, 7, 11, 16, 22, 29, 37, 46, ___?___

Write the next number in Cliff's pattern.

Ⓐ 55

Ⓑ 56

Ⓒ 57

Ⓓ 58

**15**  Deanna's class is making fabric flags. Each flag uses a 12-inch length of fabric. If there are 24 students in Deanna's class, how many feet of fabric will the class need to buy? 1 foot = 12 inches

Ⓕ 12 feet

Ⓖ 24 feet

Ⓗ 144 feet

Ⓘ 288 feet

STOP

Grade 4 • Harcourt Brace School Publishers

Name _____

## Notes

Problems that I answered correctly.

_____

_____

_____

_____

_____

_____

Problems that I did not understand.

_____

_____

_____

_____

Vocabulary that I need to learn.

_____

_____

_____

_____

**1** For a class project, Thomas drew a map of his town. Look at his map and decide which answer below tells the best way to measure the actual distance from the school to the fire station.

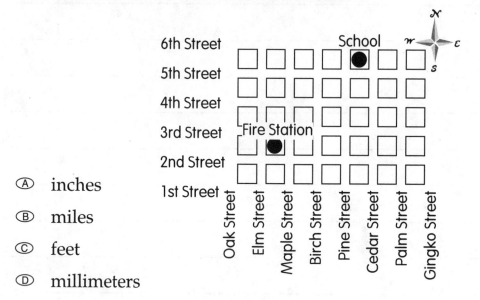

Ⓐ inches

Ⓑ miles

Ⓒ feet

Ⓓ millimeters

**2** Roberta and her classmates collected data about students' families. Their findings are shown in the Venn diagram below. Each "x" stands for a student in their class. How many students have both brothers and sisters?

Ⓕ 8

Ⓖ 4

Ⓗ 5

Ⓘ 12

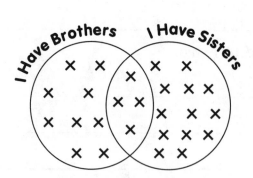

Grade 4 • Harcourt Brace School Publishers

**3** Sarah's grandmother is starting a small garden outside her apartment, shown below. About how many feet of wood edging will she need to fit around the perimeter of her garden?

Ⓕ 6 feet

Ⓖ 10 feet

Ⓗ 20 feet

Ⓘ 24 feet

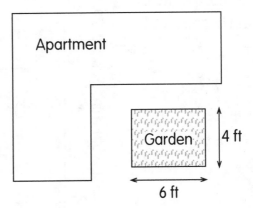

**4** Adam is 3 years older than Nick. If Nick is 15 years old, which equation below will give you Adam's age?

Ⓐ $15 + 3 = ?$

Ⓑ $15 - 3 = ?$

Ⓒ $15 \div 3 = ?$

Ⓓ $15 \times 3 = ?$

**5**

Rosie's class kept records of the daytime high temperatures in their hometown for 5 days in December. They made a line graph of their findings. For two days in a row, the temperature was the same. What was the temperature on these two days?

Ⓕ  40°

Ⓖ  44°

Ⓗ  48°

Ⓘ  50°

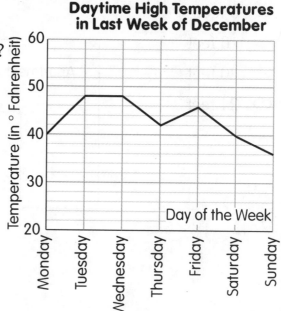

**Daytime High Temperatures in Last Week of December**

**6**

Richard and John started a chess club. There were two people at the first meeting, 4 people at the second meeting, and 8 people at the third meeting. If this pattern continues, how many people will be at the fifth meeting?

Ⓐ  14 people

Ⓑ  16 people

Ⓒ  24 people

Ⓓ  32 people

**7**

Lana is making a bead necklace. She is following a pattern. Her unfinished necklace looks like this.

O o o O o o O

She will use 34 beads in all. How many large beads will Lana need if she continues the pattern? On the lines below, explain how you solved the problem.

_____

_____

_____

_____

**8**

The students in Jeremy's fourth grade class had a contest to see who could fill a jar of beans first. Jeremy collected 50 beans. Sharon collected 100 beans. Xavier collected 125 beans. ESTIMATE how full Sharon's jar is. ESTIMATE how full Xavier's jar is compared to Jeremy's jar.

**Jeremy's Jar**   **Sharon's Jar**   **Xavier's Jar**

On the lines below, explain your reasoning.

_____

_____

_____

_____

_____

**9** Timothy surveyed his classmates about their favorite outdoor activities. Each student voted for one favorite activity. His data is shown on the list.

**Survey of Students' Favorite Outdoor Activities**

| Activity | Number of Students |
|----------|--------------------|
| soccer | 7 |
| camping | 2 |
| riding bicycles | 14 |
| skating | 5 |

On the answer sheet, make a bar graph to show the favorite outdoor activities of the students in Timothy's survey.

Then write two statements that compare the data.

Name _____

9 Make a bar graph to show the favorite outdoor activities of the students in Timothy's survey. Be sure to

- give your graph an appropriate title
- label each bar
- choose an appropriate scale
- accurately graph the data

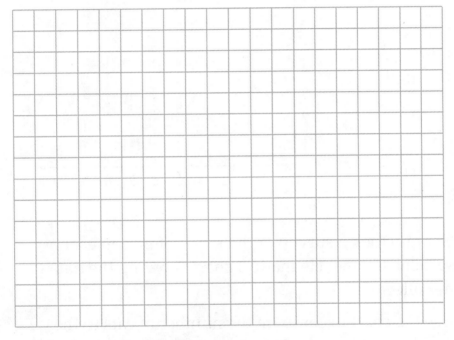

Use the information in your bar graph to write two statements that compare the data.

1. _____

_____

_____

2. _____

_____

_____

Grade 4 • Harcourt Brace School Publishers

New York Test Prep • Practice Test 3

**141**

Name _____

**10** Ben plotted points A and B on the grid below. Which of the ordered pairs below should Ben graph to make a right triangle?

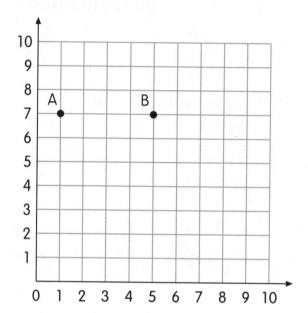

Ⓐ (6, 1)

Ⓑ (3, 8)

Ⓒ (2, 2)

Ⓓ (1, 5)

**11** Georgio took a survey of the kinds of pets in each student's home. He made a chart showing the data he collected.

Use the chart to compare the number of cats to the number of hamsters. Which of the ratios below compares the number of cats to the number of hamsters?

Ⓕ 8 to 24

Ⓖ 10 to 14

Ⓗ 24 to 8

Ⓘ 28 to 10

| Pets in Our Homes | |
|---|---|
| **Pet** | **Number** |
| Cat | 24 |
| Dog | 28 |
| Fish | 14 |
| Gerbil | 10 |
| Hamster | 8 |

Name _____

**12** Amber made this design. Patrick rotated her design. Which picture below shows the design after it was rotated?

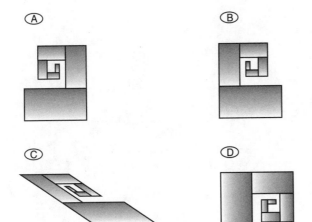

Ⓐ

Ⓑ

Ⓒ

Ⓓ

**13** A bullfrog can jump 18 inches in one jump. How far can a bullfrog travel in 4 jumps if he keeps up the same rate?

Ⓕ 4.5 inches

Ⓖ 14 inches

Ⓗ 42 inches

Ⓘ 72 inches

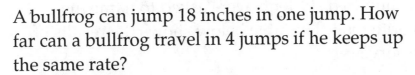

Grade 4 • Harcourt Brace School Publishers

**14** LaShondra was dismissed from school at 2:30. Immediately after school ended, LaShondra spent 15 minutes helping her teacher. Then she spent 45 minutes tutoring another student. After this, she played on the playground for half an hour. After playing, she started to walk home. What time was this?

Ⓐ 2:30

Ⓑ 3:00

Ⓒ 3:45

Ⓓ 4:00

**15** One hundred students were asked to name their favorite food. The table below shows the results of the survey.

What percent of students did *not* choose hamburger as their favorite food?

Ⓕ 15%

Ⓖ 30%

Ⓗ 70%

Ⓘ 85%

| Favorite Foods | Number of Students |
| --- | --- |
| Hamburger | 30 |
| Pizza | 45 |
| Salad | 15 |
| Soup | 10 |
| TOTAL | 100 |

STOP

Grade 4 • Harcourt Brace School Publishers

# Answer Sheet • page 1

**1** Ⓐ Ⓑ Ⓒ Ⓓ    **2** Ⓕ Ⓖ Ⓗ Ⓘ    **3** Ⓐ Ⓑ Ⓒ Ⓓ

**4** Ⓕ Ⓖ Ⓗ Ⓘ    **5** Ⓐ Ⓑ Ⓒ Ⓓ    **6** Ⓕ Ⓖ Ⓗ Ⓘ

# Answer Sheet • page 2

**7** _____

_____

_____

_____

_____

_____

_____

**8** _____

_____

_____

_____

_____

_____

_____

_____

_____

Grade 4 • Harcourt Brace School Publishers

Name _____

# Answer Sheet • page 3

**9**

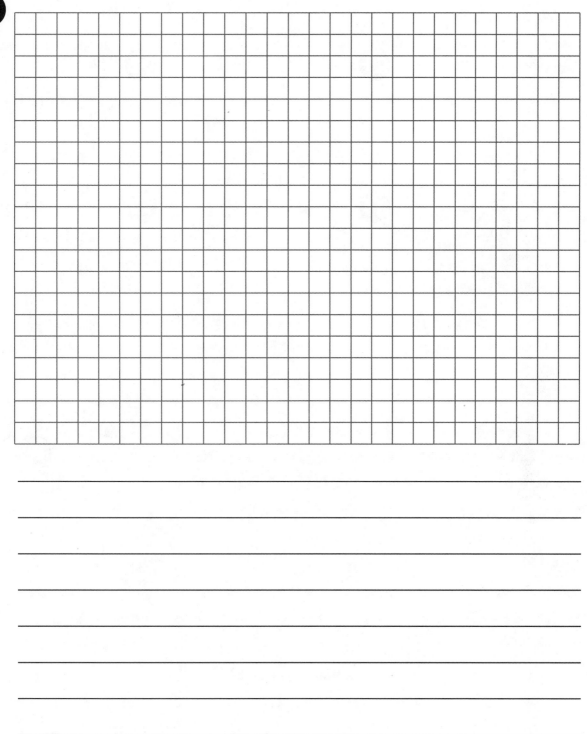

_____

_____

_____

_____

_____

_____

_____

# Answer Sheet • page 4

**10** Ⓐ Ⓑ Ⓒ Ⓓ          **11** Ⓕ Ⓖ Ⓗ Ⓘ          **12** Ⓐ Ⓑ Ⓒ Ⓓ

**13** Ⓕ Ⓖ Ⓗ Ⓘ          **14** Ⓐ Ⓑ Ⓒ Ⓓ          **15** Ⓕ Ⓖ Ⓗ Ⓘ

**STOP**

# Answer Sheet • page 1

**1** (A) (B) (C) (D)    **2** (F) (G) (H) (I)    **3** (A) (B) (C) (D)

**4** (F) (G) (H) (I)    **5** (A) (B) (C) (D)    **6** (F) (G) (H) (I)

# Answer Sheet • page 2

**7** _____

_____

_____

_____

_____

_____

_____

_____

**8** _____

_____

_____

_____

_____

_____

_____

_____

Grade 4 • Harcourt Brace School Publishers

# Answer Sheet • page 3

**9**

_____

_____

_____

_____

_____

_____

_____

Grade 4 • Harcourt Brace School Publishers

# Answer Sheet • page 4

**10** Ⓐ Ⓑ Ⓒ Ⓓ   **11** Ⓕ Ⓖ Ⓗ Ⓘ   **12** Ⓐ Ⓑ Ⓒ Ⓓ

**13** Ⓕ Ⓖ Ⓗ Ⓘ   **14** Ⓐ Ⓑ Ⓒ Ⓓ   **15** Ⓕ Ⓖ Ⓗ Ⓘ

STOP

Daily Practice

# Answer Sheet • page 1

**Practice Test____**

1 Ⓐ Ⓑ Ⓒ Ⓓ    2 Ⓕ Ⓖ Ⓗ Ⓘ    3 Ⓐ Ⓑ Ⓒ Ⓓ

4 Ⓕ Ⓖ Ⓗ Ⓘ    5 Ⓐ Ⓑ Ⓒ Ⓓ    6 Ⓕ Ⓖ Ⓗ Ⓘ

Daily Practice

**Practice Test____**

# Answer Sheet • page 2

**7** _____

_____

_____

_____

_____

_____

_____

_____

**8** _____

_____

_____

_____

_____

_____

_____

_____

Grade 4 • Harcourt Brace School Publishers

# Answer Sheet • page 3

**9**

_____

_____

_____

_____

_____

_____

_____

_____

Daily Practice

Practice Test____

# Answer Sheet • page 4

**10** Ⓐ Ⓑ Ⓒ Ⓓ     **11** Ⓕ Ⓖ Ⓗ Ⓘ     **12** Ⓐ Ⓑ Ⓒ Ⓓ

**13** Ⓕ Ⓖ Ⓗ Ⓘ     **14** Ⓐ Ⓑ Ⓒ Ⓓ     **15** Ⓕ Ⓖ Ⓗ Ⓘ

STOP

Grade 4 • Harcourt Brace School Publishers